PUBLIC SPACE AND THE CULTURE OF CHILDHOOD

For Lindsay Webb-Cornwall (1964–2002) in memory of a childhood shared.

Public Space and the Culture of Childhood

GILL VALENTINE
University of Sheffield, UK

ASHGATE

Published by
Ashgate Publishing Limited
Gower House
Croft Road
Aldershot
Hants GU11 3HR
England

Ashgate Publishing Company
Suite 420
101 Cherry Street
Burlington, VT 05401–4405
USA

Ashgate website: http://www.ashgate.com

British Library Cataloguing in Publication Data
Valentine, Gill
    Public space and the culture of childhood
    1.Children - Great Britain 2.Children - Great Britain -
    Social conditions 3.Public spaces - Social aspects - Great
    Britain
    I.Title
    305.2'3'0941

Library of Congress Cataloging-in-Publication Data
Valentine, Gill, 1965-
    Public space and the culture of childhood / Gill Valentine.
        p. cm.
    Includes bibliographical references and index.
    ISBN 0-7546-4254-2
        1. Children--Great Britain--Social conditions. 2. Children--Great Britain--Public opinion.
    3. Parents--Great Britain--Attitudes. 4. Children and the environment--Great Britain. 5.
    Public spaces--Great Britain. 6. Spatial behavior--Great Britain. I. Title.

    HQ792.G7V35 2004
    305.23'0941--dc22

                                                                    2004047615

ISBN 0 7546 4254 2

Typeset in Times Roman by N²productions
Printed and bound in Great Britain by MPG Books Ltd, Bodmin, Cornwall.

Contents

List of Tables

Acknowledgements

I am grateful to the Economic and Social Research Council for funding the research on which this book is based, award no. R.000234663. Many thanks go to John McKendrick and Leonie Kapadia who were employed as research assistants on this project; and to all the interviewees who willingly gave up their time to participate in the study.

I could not have put this manuscript together without the time afforded by a Philip Leverhulme Prize Fellowship.

I owe a huge debt to Caroline Wintersgill who commissioned this manuscript and Mary Savigar for her support in the delivery and production process. The quality of the final product is largely due to the hard work of the editorial and production team at Ashgate.

Some of the material in this book has appeared in journal articles. I am grateful to Carfax and Pion for permission to reproduce these extracts. If any proper acknowledgement has not been made I would invite copyright holders to inform me of the oversight.

Finally, thanks and much love is due to my friends, family and cats for seeing me through the various stages of research and writing.

Chapter 1

Childhood in Crisis?

In the summer of 2002 two British schoolgirls, aged ten, went missing from Soham, Cambridgeshire, a peaceful rural town, and were subsequently found murdered. Their disappearance and tragic deaths attracted media attention around the world, and was marked by public mourning, the like of which had not been seen before. During the same year two boys, who had abducted and murdered the toddler Jamie Bulger in Liverpool, Merseyside in 1993, while only ten years old, came of age and were released from juvenile custody. The decision to release them rather than send them to an adult prison, and to provide them with new identities and protection to start a new life provoked an equally loud media and public response. These two examples of childhood in the UK capture twin contemporary fears about children as both at risk in public space, and as a cause of trouble in public space. This book is about these fears and the extent to which childhood might be considered in crisis.

The binary conceptualisation of children as both vulnerable and in need of protection, yet also potentially menacing and dangerous have a long history. The remainder of this chapter traces some of these debates about this moral landscape of childhood. This outline is not intended to be a detailed historical account, but rather seeks to draw out some of the key arguments that have characterised diverse understandings of what it means to be a child. The chapter then introduces academic understandings of the family, and of the concepts of space and community, before going on to outline the research about contemporary childhood and space that is used as evidence in the following chapters. Finally, this chapter outlines the structure and content of the remainder of the book.

Defining Childhood: Angels and Devils

The history of both childhood and parent-child relations are complex and contradictory. Aries (1962) (perhaps the most famous child historian) argues that in the Middle Ages children were seen as miniature adults, rather than as being in a distinct social category defined by biological age, and consequently no special provisions were made for them. Once children demonstrated capabilities such as reason, concentration and strength they took on adult roles including domestic service, apprenticeships, and education. It was only in the sixteenth century that children started to be defined in opposition to adults, and from the Enlightenment onwards, that this understanding of children – as a particular class of person – came to dominate our social imaginations (Jenks 1996). In other words, childhood is a social invention. As James and Jenks (1996) argue '[t]he biological facts of infancy are but the raw material upon which cultures work to fashion a particular version of "being a child".' This is a process 'suffused with moral assumptions' (Jordanova 1989: 4). Most notably, two contrasting narratives have come to dominate the way that we think about children. Jenks (1996) labels these Dionysian and Apollonian.

Dionysian understandings of childhood regard children as the inheritors of original sin, as possessing animal-like instincts: a wildness. Children are regarded as developing towards adulthood out of this state of primal animality. This is a conception of the child as a little savage or devil who is inherently unruly, and troublesome but who can be disciplined and socialised into adult ways of behaviour. It dominated understandings of childhood in the seventeenth century. For example, Takanishi (1978: 11) observes how at this time, '[t]he child was viewed in the child rearing literature as innately sinful but potentially redeemable through the constant and determined efforts of his [sic] parents.'

By the end of the seventeenth century a group of academics known as the Cambridge Platonists (including Ralph Cudworth and Richard Cumberland) began to propose a re-evaluation of childhood (Sommerville 1982). They advanced the notion that children possessed an innate goodness that is then corrupted by the social world they grow up in. According to Sommerville (1982: 121) '[t]his went even beyond the notion of the innocence of the baptised child. For "innocence" may only mean a neutral state – neither positively bad nor positively good. These men postulated principles of innate "sympathy" or "benevolence" that formed the basis of conscience and sociable behaviour'. This is the Apollonian understanding of childhood.

What followed in the eighteenth century was a debate on the nature of childhood in which Apollonian and Dionysian understandings of childhood were openly contested. On the one hand, there was a strong romanticisation of original innocence amongst contemporary novelists and poets, such as Blake, Coleridge and Wordsworth. Rousseau's *Emile* (1762), for example, explores the story of a boy growing up and how he develops naturally from birth under the guidance of a wise tutor. It is a sympathetic and sentimental portrayal of childhood that is often credited with marking the transition from the Dark Age of demonised childhood to a period of enlightened concern (Sommerville, 1982).

On the other hand, at the same time there was a backlash against the pro-child lobby. With the late eighteenth century rocked by the European revolutions and instability, notions of the rights of children were challenged in the UK by conservative writers anxious for an ordered society (Hendrick 1990). Among them Maria Edworth argued 'Is it not a fundamental error to consider children as innocent beings, whose little weaknesses may, perhaps, want some correction, rather than as beings who bring into the world a corrupt nature and evil dispositions, which it should be the great end of education to rectify?' (Robertson 1976: 421).

However, gradually there was a fragmented emergence of the dominant notion of childhood innocence and the innate goodness of the child, violated by an evil society (Takanishi 1978). This view, that children began as 'noble, unselfish and joyous creatures until society crushed or corrupted their spirit' (Takanishi 1978: 11) was also adopted by Victorians. It was, however, a very elite notion that co-existed in the nineteenth century with a period of industrial capitalism characterised by the brutal exploitation of child labour in factories.

This led to growing concern amongst some middle class reformers who wanted to regulate certain forms of child labour. Part of this concern was based on a conceptualisation of children as a natural resource that needed to be nurtured and conserved but more pragmatically it also derived from a fear that 'the brutalisation of ["working class"] children was contributing to the dehumanisation of social class' (Hendrick 1990: 41) and that this would lead to moral and social instability. Education was perceived to be one way to instil discipline, respect for order and punctuality in working class children. According to May (1973: 12) 'Schools were to act as "moral hospitals" and provide corrective training'. In this way education not only imposed middle class values on the general population, but also had the added advantage for the middle-classes of helping them to control their own children (Schnell 1979: 17). Education became a fundamental process through which adulthood was achieved, a marker of the transition to adulthood (Postman 1982, Archard 1993). Paradoxically at the same time education also signalled a move to a recognition of childhood as a special period of time separated off from the responsibilities of adulthood.

Ideologically related to the emergence of universal education was the construction of a notion of juvenile delinquency. In the early nineteenth century there was no separate legal system for the young and prisons increasingly became full of children. It was argued that these institutions were corrupting young people – and to coin a wonderful phrase of this period – 'vomiting them back into society', provoking growing concerns about delinquency. Takanishi (1978: 13) describes how '[r]agged unsupervised children roved the streets in small bands, sometimes stealing and breaking store windows'. This then was a period when the middle class saw working class children as a moral and physical pestilence, likening them to packs of 'ownerless dogs' (May 1973: 7). Above all it was feared that these children without a childhood were a threat to those that had one (Schnell 1979: 23).

Gradually judicial self-interest, the need to reduce prison costs and a growing awareness of children's rights led to the first statutory distinction between adults and children in the form of legislation recognising juvenile delinquency. This legislation identified children as not necessarily responsible for their own actions and as requiring care and protection. When parents failed to provide this physical and moral care the State, the legislation decreed, had the right to act *in loco parentis* (May 1973: 12).

Reformatory schools were introduced as a way of remoralizing delinquent young people. These were, according to Ploszajska (1994: 413) 'the very embodiment of contemporary belief in the latent power of the social and physical environment to influence behaviour'. Boys' reformatories were established in rural sites, the antithesis of the corrupting environment of the city; while institutions for girls were located in suburban areas reflecting the domesticity that girls were expected to aspire to (Ploszajska 1994). Likewise, the development of the playground movement in Cambridge, Massachusetts, US, at the beginning of the twentieth century also reflected a desire on behalf of the middle classes to gain control over children and stop them running wild. In particular, middle class Americans at this time were concerned about the need for growing numbers of immigrant children to be assimilated into the national way of life (Gagen 1998, 2000). Playground regimes were established with the intention of creating appropriately gendered US citizens and correcting anti-social behaviour. Notably, they attempted to refocus the 'natural instinct' of boys to form street gangs into team sports in the playground.

Through legislation (in the late nineteenth and early twentieth centuries) and more critically the introduction of mass schooling (and later the National Health Service), Hendrick argues that the mythical condition of childhood was popularised and gradually a universal notion of childhood emerged. Steedman describes the changes which took place between 1870 and 1930 as a 'profound transformation in the economic and sentimental value of children' (Steedman 1990: 63). The economic value of children went down as there was a shift away from the child as labourer, towards a conceptualisation of the child as dependant. This was accompanied by a parallel change in family life and by new (literary, artistic and photographic) representations of childhood (Steedman 1990).

The development of welfarist protectionism in the twentieth and twenty-first centuries, variously improving children's educational, legal, environmental, physical conditions and life-opportunities and the greater resources invested in children by parents (e.g. child oriented toys, fashions, foods, entertainments) have further fostered representations of childhood as a time of innocence and vulnerability when children are in need of protection from the adult world (Stainton Rogers and Stainton Rogers 1992).

During the twentieth century the length of time young people are legally defined as dependent on their parent(s) has been extended by a post-war increase in the school leaving age from 14 to 16 and more recently by changes in welfare provision which, for example, have driven up the age at which teenagers can first claim welfare benefits in the UK from 16 to 18. (Although paradoxically others, such as Neil Postman, argue that the length of childhood is contracting, with the media, fashion industry and technology all accused of blurring the boundaries between adults and children.)

In the twentieth century, 'the family', particularly the mother has been conceived as crucial to the development and well-being of children. It is primarily mothers who are held responsible for their children turning out 'right' (Hardyment 1990, Phoenix and Woollett 1991), as law abiding, 'mature' citizens (Walkerdine and Lucey 1989). As Phoenix and Woollett (1991: 18), argue 'mothers in the UK are expected to be guardians of the liberal democracy by bringing their children up to be self regulating' (Phoenix and Woollett 1991: 18). These idealised constructions of what it means to be a 'good' mother – which are primarily white and middle class – are particularly apparent in childcare and parenting manuals as well as everyday discourses (Marshall 1991). Working class mothers, single parents and mothers from minority ethnic groups who are perceived or assumed to deviate from these white, middle class 'norms' (Phoenix and Woollett 1991) are frequently accused by populist politicians and media of producing unruly or 'dangerous children'. Yet numerous studies have demonstrated that such accusations have no foundation (Walkerdine and Lucey 1989).

The innate innocence and vulnerability of the child has also been reinforced in the late twentieth century through public discourses about stranger-dangers and child abuse (Cream 1993). As Kitizinger (1990: 158) points out 'the victim is the child – and ultimately, childhood itself is at issue ... The concern is therefore, not just about the assault on an individual child but with the attack upon, and defence of, childhood itself (that institution and ideal which exists independently from, and sometimes in spite of, actual flesh and blood children)'. And she goes on to argue that '[i]ndeed, the sexual abuse of a child is often referred to as the "theft" or "violation" of childhood'.

The twentieth century has therefore witnessed the emergence of a conception of a coherent 'universal' childhood. Namely, that a child is temporally set apart from the adult world (although there are multiple and conflicting definitions of the age at which this division occurs); that children are innocent, incompetent and vulnerably dependent (on both parent(s) and the State); and that childhood is a happy and free time, lacking responsibilities. This is, however, the dominant imagining of childhood rather than reality experienced by most children. The experience of childhood has never been universal, rather what it means to be a particular age intersects with other identities so that experiences of poverty, disability, ill health, homelessness, being taken into care, or having to look after a sick parent have all denied many children this idealised time of innocence and dependence (James and Jenks 1996). Likewise 'growing up' has been based on the false assumption that social development follows on from physical growth and that it marks a transition from simplicity to complexity and from irrationality to rationality. The reality once again is that many children have to demonstrate maturity and responsibility at an early age (for example, children who act as interpreters for their parents); whereas some adults are perpetually immature.

The twentieth-century notion of universal childhood is further complicated by the invention in the 1950s of the teenager. The focus in this period on consumption, style and leisure led to the emergence of a range of commodities and facilities (discos, record shops, fashion magazines and so on) targeted at this new market niche. At the same time links were made between youth sub cultures (particularly working class adolescents), juvenile crime and 'gang' violence. As Hebdige (1988: 30) explains '[t]he two image clusters, the bleak portraits of juvenile offenders and exuberant cameos of teenage life reverberate, alternate and sometimes they get crossed'. Teenagers therefore lie awkwardly placed between childhood and adulthood: sometimes constructed and represented as 'innocent' 'children' in need of protection from adult sexuality, violence and commercial exploitation; at other times represented as articulating adult vices of drink, drugs and violence. Indeed, some commentators have argued that the growing commodification of youth is eroding childhood as a distinctive stage, as young people take on all of the trappings of adulthood from clothing to consumption (which are associated with the loss of innocence) at an earlier and earlier age (Postman 1982). Diduck (1999), for example, suggests that the increasing numbers of children acting in unchildlike ways, that is beyond the control and comprehension of adults, is causing a contemporary troubling about what constitutes childhood and prompting anger and fear.

In summary then, the past four centuries have witnessed the construction and (re)production of different accounts of childhood in which, despite the complex and multiple realities of children's lives, childhood has been understood through the oppositional discourses of 'angels' and 'devils'. Although the Apollonian notion of childhood emerged after the Dionysian notion it has never entirely supplanted the former. Rather, contradictory versions of childhood co-exist and continue to be mobilised. At different moments one or other of these simplified narratives of childhood appears to dominate the popular imagination (Stainton Rogers and Stainton Rogers 1992). Like other fashions however, the opposite binary representation of childhood (although always present in children's complex and diverse experiences) is periodically rediscovered (Stainton Rogers and Stainton Rogers 1992). The remainder of this book explores the ways that these different ideas are being mobilised in contemporary Europe and North America in relation to debates about children's role and place in public space.

The 'Post-Modern' Family

Just as there is contemporary anxiety about the changing nature of childhood, so too the family has also been called into question. Writers such as Popenoe (1988) have argued that the family is in decline. Using data from Sweden that shows marriage rates at an all time low and rising divorce rates, he suggests that the family is losing its social function and power. Statistics from other countries reveal a similar pattern of marriage breakdown. For example, whilst in 1950 three-fifths of US households were composed of a male wage earner and a female homemaker, by 1987 the number of households fitting this description had dropped to only 7 per cent (Stacey 1990). Nearly 1 in 2 US children, and 1 in 3 British children will experience the break-up of their birth family during their childhood (Jensen 1994). In these situations children usually continue to live with their mothers (even when the parents have joint custody). Although many fathers retain some form of contact with their children, research suggests that nearly a quarter of fathers have no economic or personal contact with their children after separation, producing what has been termed the 'feminization of childhood' (Jensen 1994: 74).

Other commentators however, have challenged Poponoe's conclusions that such patterns mark the death of the family (e.g. Silva and Smart 1999, Morgan 1999). Rather, they argue that while family forms may be moving away from traditional notions of 'proper' nuclear families, and some practices within the family may be changing, 'families remain a crucial relational entity playing a fundamental part in the intimate life of and connections between individuals' (Silva and Smart 1999: 5). What is changing is the way that people are 'doing' families. In particular, the traditional nuclear family with a male breadwinner and a female homemaker (taking sole responsibility for childcare) as a particular form of doing family is in decline.

Although marriage rates may be falling and traditional nuclear families breaking up, most adults continue to live in partnerships, or aspire to these forms of relationships. It just means that they are no longer necessarily bound together legally but rather are together through choice (Stacey 1990, Weeks et al. 2000). These forms of living arrangements include: co-habiting partners (with or without children) who are not legally married; lone parents; same-sex partnerships; part-time relationships; relationships that are maintained between different homes, sometimes over large geographical distances; and so on (see for example: Chandler 1991, Weeks et al. 1999, Smart 1999). Beck and Beck-Gernsheim (2002: 98) explain '[T]his does not mean that the traditional family is simply disappearing. But it is losing the monopoly it had for so long. Its quantitative significance is declining as new forms of living appear and spread'. These 'post-modern families' (Stacey 1990) or post families (Beck and Beck-Gernsheim 2002), as they have been variously described, may differ from traditional nuclear families in terms of their degree of obligation or permanence but they are still characterised by their members' commitment to intimacy, sharing resources, and maintaining responsibilities for each other, albeit in different ways (Bernardes 1987, Finch and Mason 1993, Silva and Smart 1999).

Given these social changes it is intensely difficult to retain the term 'family' in academic writing, because of the ideological baggage associated with it. Notably, it can imply 'a firm, unchanging entity, always similar in shape and content' (Thorne 1987: 4) that does not adequately capture the complex, fluid and multiple ways that contemporary people organise their lives. However, family is employed in this book, not to refer to traditional nuclear families alone, but rather to describe the many and varied household arrangements which make up the 'post modern family'.

Space and Community

In the late nineteenth and early twentieth centuries space was conceived by cartographers, and geographers as something to be investigated, mapped and classified (a process enhanced by the development of instrumental, mathematical and graphical techniques). After the Second World War this emphasis on the description of uniqueness was replaced by a concern with similarity. Specifically, geographers became concerned with uncovering universal spatial laws to understand the way the world worked. The focus was on spatial order and the use of quantitative methods to explain and predict human patterns of behaviour. Space was conceptualised as an objective physical surface with specific fixed characteristics upon which social identities and categories were mapped out. It was in effect understood as the container of social relations and events.

Subsequently, geographers began to recognise that space was not simply an objective structure but a social experience imbued with interwoven layers of social meaning. Radical approaches to geography, most notably those inspired by Marxism, also began to recognise space as the product of social forces, observing that different societies use and organise space in different ways; and to explain the processes through which social differences become spatial patterns of inequalities (Smith 1990). In the late twentieth and early twenty-first centuries geographers' engagement with postmodernism has also produced a new sensitivity to 'the myriad variations that exist between the many "sorts" of human beings ... and to recognise (and in some ways represent) the very different inputs and experiences these diverse populations have into, and of, "socio-spatial" processes' (Cloke et al. 1991: 171).

Space is no longer therefore understood as having particular fixed characteristics. Nor is it regarded as being merely a backdrop for social relations, a pre-existing terrain which exists outside of, or frames everyday life. Rather, space is understood to play an active role in the constitution and reproduction of social identities and vice versa social identities, meanings and relations are recognised as producing material and symbolic or metaphorical spaces. As such Massey (1999: 283) explains that space:

> is the product of the intricacies and the complexities, the interlockings and the non-interlockings, of relations from the unimaginably cosmic to the intimately tiny. And precisely because it is the product of relations, relations which are active practices, material and embedded, practices which have to be carried out, space is always in a process of becoming. It is always being made.

This conceptualisation frames the way that the concepts of 'public' space, 'private' space and 'community' are used and understood in this volume.

The notion of 'community' has a long and contested history within geography and urban sociology. In particular, in terms of theorizing the decline of neighbourhood community; questioning the extent to which the term has analytical value because it means so many different things to so many different people; and in terms of critiquing it as an exclusionary concept (e.g. Young 1990, Silk 1999, Valentine 2001). Despite these academic debates it is a term that continues to have meaning to a lot of people in everyday life. In this book, community is conceptualised not as a stable, fixed, measureable entity but rather in Anderson's (1983) terms as a structure of meaning. In his book *Imagined Communities* he argued that communities are imagined because people often carry a deep sense of communion or shared identity with others in their minds even though they may never meet all their fellow members and there may be inequalities or differences between them. However, although communities may be imagined at the same time they are not idealist because these imaginings are grounded in specific social, economic and political circumstances (Rose 1990). As such communities are perhaps best defined as 'a group of people bound together by some kind of belief stemming from particular historical and geographical circumstances in their own solidarity' (Rose 1990: 426). They can be place or neighbourhood based but equally they can operate across a range of different spaces and scales.

The Research

The findings presented in this book are based on material collected as part of a two-year study of parental concerns about childrens' use of public space, funded by the Economic and Social Research Council.

The research canvassed the opinions and experiences of parents with a child aged between 8 and 11 years old. This age group was selected as this is the stage when children begin to venture beyond the immediate vicinity of the home environment and thus neighbourhood play becomes a reality. The study consisted of several stages.

First, a self-completion questionnaire with cover letter and return envelope was distributed to 1000 parents through primary schools. This included 75 questions, divided into seven sections, that explored the parents' attitudes to: the local area, the child's play, the child's travel to school, the child's play through time, their concerns for their child and asked for biographical information about all household members. Parents were asked to give answers to the survey only in relation to the child who had been given the questionnaire at school and not to include other children in the household. Nearly 400 questionnaires were completed and returned.

The research adopted an environmental approach to sampling in a stratified purposive framework. Census data was used to identify possible areas, whose suitability was then verified by field survey. Thus, the implications of residing in particular types of area could be estimated (area analysis) and the likelihood of reaching particular groups of the population would be increased (individual level analysis). A core-control matrix was devised to ensure that the analytical objectives for area level analysis could be met. Nine areas were selected on the basis of social class, child demography, and macro-geographical environment. These included metropolitan, non metropolitan and rural areas in Cheshire, Derbyshire, Greater Manchester and Yorkshire.[1] They have been given the pseudonyms of Moulton (a middle class, modern private estate), Thorpe (a working-class local authority housing area), Ranwell (a working class local authority estate), Tabor Green (an area of private middle class housing), Stocksfield (a mixed class area with a modern private housing estate adjoining a local authority estate), Hunters Bridge (a middle class commuter village of modern housing developed around a former rural village), Granton (a working class private estate and local authority housing in a rural town), Wheldale (a mixed class rural village of private housing, a small local authority estate and farms) and Shenford (a mixed class area of private and local authority housing) (see Table 1.1).

Response rates to the questionnaire were favourable. On average 40 per cent of parents responded to the survey, with the response rates in different neighbourhoods ranging from 25 per cent to 62 per cent. In common with other surveys of this type, higher returns were received from middle class areas. However, the key point is that the profile of respondents closely matched that of the parental population for each individual area, in other words, the database comprises a representative sample.

Second, on the basis of the responses to the questionnaire, 70 parent(s) were selected for interview (including parents from affluent and more deprived areas; from areas with a high, medium or low proportion of children among the local population). The majority of those interviewed were white, ten households were British South Asian Muslims. The interviews were used to develop issues explored in the survey, to cover additional themes of (often local) importance that were not addressed in the questionnaire; and to explore the complexities and contradictions in parents' attitudes and behaviour. The interviews considered not only parental attitudes towards the child given the questionnaire at school but also other children (older and younger) in the household and hence also explored how parents' attitudes to children's play varies according to a child's gender, age and position in the 'family'.

In the third stage of the research ethnographic work was carried out with police and teachers involved in educating children about personal safety. Finally, focus group[2] discussions were conducted with children about their experiences of public space and how they get round the spatial restrictions imposed on them by adults.

All the methods were successfully piloted before being implemented in the research proper. All the interviews and focus groups were transcribed and analysed using conventional social science techniques. Quotations taken from these transcripts to illustrate points made in this book are verbatim, ellipsis dots indicate that an edit has been made.

Table 1.1   The Research Locations

Study Location (pseudonym)	Geographical Environment[1]	Socio-Economic Status	Housing Type	% of Children in the Area[2]
Moulton	Urban metropolitan borough	Middle class	Modern private estate	Average
Thorpe	Urban metropolitan borough	Working class	Local authority housing	Average
Ranwell	Urban metropolitan borough	Working class	Local authority estate	High
Tabor Green	Urban metropolitan borough	Middle class	Private housing	Low
Stocksfield	Urban non metropolitan	Mixed class	Adjoining private estate & local authority estate	Average
Hunters Bridge	Commuter village	Middle class	Private estate & private housing	Average
Granton	Rural town	Working class	Local authority housing & private estate	Average
Wheldale	Rural village	Mixed class	Private housing, some local authority houses & farms	Average
Shenford	Urban metropolitan borough	Mixed class	Private housing & local authority housing	Average

Source: Valentine and McKendrick 1997.

[1] Settlement classifications are taken from the OPCS Census of Population.

[2] Ranwell has the lowest proportion of adults of all electoral wards in Greater Manchester (40.5% of the population are under 16), in contrast Tabor Green has one of the highest adult populations (26.5% of the population are aged under 16). The average is 30.5%.

The Content and Structure of This Book

Chapter Two focuses on contemporary fears about children as vulnerable to 'stranger-dangers' in public space. It maps the geography of these fears and considers how potential dangers are represented to parents through the media in ways which demonise particular 'others' and construct particular spaces as safe or dangerous. The chapter concludes by examining how in trying to relay messages to children about sexual threats while maintaining their 'innocence', adults (re)produce an erroneous message that public space is dangerous while private space represents safety. The concepts of 'risk' and the 'risk society' underpins much of this discussion.

The following chapter draws attention to the way that in such protectionist approaches to children it is impossible to separate out the construction of childhood from the construction of what it means to be a 'good' parent. It therefore examines the production of local geographies of parenting and considers gender differences, both in terms of mothers' and fathers' roles in managing children's use of space in different 'family' forms, and in terms of their attitudes to sons' versus daughters' safety.

In Chapter Four the focus switches onto how parents' general under-standings of children's competence to negotiate public space safely, and their ideals about how children's spatial boundaries are translated into practice in the context of the realities of everyday domestic life. Here consideration is given to children as active social agents in their own lives who negotiate and contest understandings of their 'competence' and spatial freedoms with their parents. The chapter concludes by reflecting on parallels between parents' fears for children in outdoor public space, and emerging fears about children's safety on-line in cyberspace.

Chapter Five examines the consequences of parents' protectionist cultures for young children's use of space. The material presented suggests that there has been a retreat from the street with children increasingly spending their leisure time engaged in institutionalised activities rather than independent free play. This experience of childhood is compared to parents' memories of their own 'outdoor' childhoods. At the same time attention is also drawn to the unequal opportunities that children of different socio-economic back-grounds have to experience institutionalised leisure and free play, and the social consequences of these differences in opportunity.

In Chapter Six the focus switches from the vulnerability of young children to adults' attitudes towards teenagers in public space. It is argued that young people are often perceived to disrupt the moral order of the street. In this climate of panic about 'dangerous children', adults (parents, the police, the State, the media and so on) appear to be articulating a need for greater spatial controls to be exerted over young people in order to maintain the boundaries between 'us' and 'them'. In other words, underlying adults' contemporary anxieties about 'dangerous' children appears to be an assumption that the streets belong to adults and that children should only be permitted into public spaces when they have been socialised into appropriate 'adult' ways of behaving and using space. This opens up the issue of whether young people have a right to (re)claim the streets for themselves or whether the streets should be an adult defined and controlled space to which children are granted free access only when they have been culturally assimilated by adults. It also connects to wider debates about the decline of truly public space.

Chapter Seven draws together the ideas outlined in all of the previous chapters to evaluate the extent of the crisis of childhood and reflect on how it might be tackled. It argues that adults need to listen to the voice of children and young people, and reflects on notions of children's rights and status as citizens within the context of policy and planning. It concludes by outlining an agenda for more participatory measures to include children in planning public space and to promote children's participation and citizenship.

Throughout the book there is an attempt to maintain a recognition that children are not an undifferentiated class and to draw attention to the plurality of childhoods in terms of age, gender, socio-economic class, family form and so on.

Notes

1 During the course of the interviews some participants disclosed confidential information about local incidents of child abuse, sensitive disputes between parents and some children talked about things they did not want adults to know about. Consequently the precise locations of the research sites have been withheld in order to help protect the anonymity of those involved. Any names of people or places referred to in quotations are pseudonyms.
2 Focus groups, held in youth clubs and schools, were carried out with children in single sex and mixed groups. I am grateful to Leonie Kapadia, a research assistant on this project, for her help in setting up and facilitating these discussions.

Chapter 2

Terror Talk: Geographies of Fear

This chapter explores the construction and mobilisation of parental fears for children's safety in public space. It begins by looking at where and why parents are most fearful for their children's safety and by considering their risk assessment and management. In particular, it focuses on stranger-danger discourses, arguing that global reporting of violent crimes against children – terror talk – may distort local fears by heightening parents' awareness of extreme and rare events causing them to restrict their children's use of space excessively. Paradoxically therefore, as people's knowledge of the world expands, so their children's experiences of their local worlds contract. The chapter then goes on to focus on the way parents' and schools' squeamishness about talking about the body and sexuality with children results in a crude message of public space equals danger; versus private space equals safety being fed to children through educational programmes and campaigns. This message enables parents and other agencies to warn children about potential danger while robbing it of any sexual content. At the same time 'terror talk' represents the male body as saturated with threat and so contributes to shaping the way that adults and children relate to each other and (re)produce public space.

The Geography of Parental Fears

The majority of the parents surveyed identified primary school aged children to be most at risk of abduction (45 per cent), followed by traffic accidents (34 per cent). Only 1 per cent of parents identified their children as at risk from accidents in the home. There is a geography to these perceptions of fear. Most parents believe that children are likely to be snatched by strangers (63 per cent) rather than adults known to them (16 per cent) or estranged parents (10 per cent); and that these abductions are most likely to occur in public parks (60 per cent), followed by shopping centres (34 per cent), playgrounds (33 per cent) and outside school (6 per cent).[1] These findings are replicated by other surveys in UK and North America, that all show that fear of attack (by paedophiles or murderers) is seen as the single most significant risk to children outside the home (Blakely, 1994, Hood et al. 1996, Kelley et al. 1997). In the UK 19,500 offenders are currently registered under the Sex Offenders Act of 1997 (Foreign and Commonwealth Office 2004). This mother's description of her fears for her daughter's safety captures the micro geographies of risk in public space:

Mother: She has boundaries here beyond which she will not go. I mean she's allowed to go to the post box which is 100 yards down the road and she's allowed to go up to one of the closes further up. But there are boundaries. She said [her daughter] 'could I go to such and such?', but I said 'no, that's too far'. She's got a friend that lives further down but she has to pass the blocks of flats and I am always apprehensive there because it's sort of single people that live there, it isn't parents generally with children and because there's so many people coming in and out there is a place where people could hang round. You see we've got the woods just behind us and they're not – she's not allowed to go in the woods which is – you know causes her real grief cos they'd love to go. And I'd love to be able to let them go and wander through the woods and pick bluebells but it's just too dangerous. I mean there's people go down there and walk the dogs and people go down there fishing. I'm sure they're perfectly nice people but I don't think you can trust anybody these days ('middle class', commuter village, Cheshire).

Such fears are exacerbated for British Asian parents by the vulnerability of their children to racially motivated interpersonal violence, especially in late teenage and early adult years. These fears are borne out by the evidence of a number of studies (Keith 1995, Toon and Qureshi 1995) including the work of Watt and Stenson (1998) in which they argue that white youths actively use violence to exclude other ethnic groups from their neighbourhoods in what Hesse et al. (1992: 171) label 'white territorialism'.

Differences in parental fears amongst those interviewed for this study were also evident in relation to place. Whilst parents from all the different research locations expressed general concerns about children's vulnerability to abduction, they also expressed more specific local concerns about their children relating to the social and physical characteristics of their own neighbourhoods. In one neighbourhood parental fears were mediated by a problem with local teenage gangs; in another traffic problems and the design and layout of the housing structured their local concerns. These are not uniquely urban anxieties. Despite the fact that the countryside is popularly imagined to be a safe, predictable and harmonious place, isolated from city problems, rural parents argued that their local landscape is a honey pot for urban strangers, such as walkers and tourists, as well as mobile communities such as New Age Travellers and more 'traditional' gypsies. This uncertainty about 'who' may be in the village and surrounding fields means that rural communities also have their own specific local stranger-danger concerns as these parents explain:

Mother: I mean Slades Lane where the fields are up there, you get a lot of people walking around with their dogs and you never just know who's about. Even when I'm taking the cows up there and I'm walking back – all the wind's blowing at you I always like look behind me because you can't hear anyone coming up behind you … so I won't let them go and play up there. Because we had a load of New Age Travellers up the lane there a couple of years ago and they were there for months. So you never know who's going to suddenly appear around the corner. So it's because of strangers I don't let them go up there ('middle class', rural village, Derbyshire).

Mother: We are very cautious aren't we [to her husband] because you just never know. I mean I suppose you, you are influenced by what you hear on the news because you hear you know, you think you're safer in the country, but then there're, there may always be someone lurking around, you get so many tourists here and walkers.
Father: … I don't think you can actually tell so I mean I suppose we are both careful but, um, I don't know. I work you know, I work in Manchester and London and it never fails to amaze me the sort of people that you see around there. And then I think well these people could even be where we live, you know, they're still around and, er, so I think if anything we're over cautious with Jack ('middle class,' rural village, Derbyshire).

The popular perception amongst parents is that children's safety has deteriorated since they were young. Three out of five of the parents surveyed claimed to have had more freedom to play outside during their own childhoods than their children do (a point that is developed in Chapter Five) and believe that as a consequence their children are missing out on social and play opportunities. This mother explains:

Mother: I think children's safety's got worse, you know, you can't let 'em out in the streets. I mean years ago we weren't, me mum would say we weren't frightened to let you [her and siblings] out, you know whereas I say I won't let these in the front garden, so um obviously that's got a lot worse ('working class', non-metropolitan town, Cheshire).

It is a view that is often replicated in the press. Writing in *The Times* newspaper, this journalist contrasts his own memories of an idyllic rural childhood with what he imagines to be the state of contemporary childhood:

I often went fishing, sometimes on my own, usually with a friend. We would cycle seven or eight miles out of the city in the direction of Comber and there fish for pike in the local river. All that concerned us was a speculative bull that occasionally strayed into the same field. We ate our sandwiches, wrestled in the grass and swapped stories about the idiots we were forced to go to school with. No one approached us, or if they did it was only to say hello and ask if we'd caught anything. At no stage did we feel remotely at risk. All that has just gone now. Childhood over the past 20 years seems to have become as fraught with danger as it always has been for the young of other species. There are predators about, ready to molest and kill (Ellis 1995: 13).

Yet despite these popular imaginings, the number of children killed each year in the UK is both statistically exceptionally low (on average fewer than six children a year are murdered by strangers) and relatively unchanged year on year. Indeed, the rate of child abuse deaths has barely altered in

30 years (NSPCC 2004) despite the fact that the number of people charged or cautioned for child pornography offences has risen by 1500 per cent since 1988, largely due to the increase in material available on the Internet (BBC 2004). While there has been a general increase in recorded violence against children, the majority of perpetrators are parents/relatives, and the children most at risk are not those old enough to play independently in public space but rather are babies aged under one year old (Scott et al. 1998). Indeed, most paedophiles, contrary to the popular stereotype of the 'pervert' stalking and abducting children in public space, actually abuse their own children, stepchildren or others with whom they have a family relationship (National Criminal Intelligence Service 2002). The picture is similar in North America where the high profile given to the abduction (and murder) of children by strangers also distracts from the low number of actual cases. Non custodial parents perpetrate most abductions here and more children runaway than are kidnapped. Although, the National Center for Missing and Exploited Children, established with Justice Department backing, has put the number of stranger abductions as high as 4,000 to 20,000 (Spitzer 1986). However, these figures are believed to include incidents where a child was abducted only momentarily (Spitzer 1986). In sum then, children are more at risk in private space from people that they know (Cream 1993, Kitzinger 1990, NSPCC 2000) and from domestic hazards and accidents (Roberts, Smith and Lloyd 1992); yet parental fears imagine a geography of danger from strangers in public space.

Risk Assessment

It is widely acknowledged that we are witnessing an historical transformation in society. The industrial era, which has been characterised by rationality, scientific knowledge, social hierarchies and tradition, is being challenged by a new modernity in which traditional ideas and expectations about social relations are being reworked. There has been a weakening of class ties, a decline in the reliance on authorities such as the church, and an explosion of information. Released from the constraints and social norms of tradition, it is argued that individuals are now freer to choose between a range of options in the pursuit of their own happiness. However, this very proliferation and diffusion of knowledge, means that modern society seems inherently more risky than previous ones (Beck 1992). The invisibility and unpredictability of contemporary risk creates a society of uncertainty: dubbed by Beck (1992) 'the risk society.'

While risks may be produced by social conditions, we as individuals are expected to monitor and manage them. As such risk assessment and decision-making are increasingly important features of daily life (Beck 1992, Giddens 1992). Risk assessment is one of the ways we make the world more manageable. Yet, with this freedom to make choices also comes potential societal blame if our probability calculations are wrong (Douglas 1992). Individuals are expected to accept personal responsibility for any negative consequences or misfortunes that accrue from their reflexivity and choices. It is a process that has been termed 'individualisation' (Beck 1992, Beck and Beck-Gernsheim 2002).

Despite being very concerned about their children's safety in public space, most parents who participated in this research also acknowledged that the probability of their own child being snatched is low or fairly low (65 per cent). Yet, despite this recognition most still opt to restrict their children's play in public space because the consequences of not doing so and losing a child make the risk not worthwhile. This reflects in part, both the value of children in contemporary society, and the extent to which parents feel responsible for their risk management. These fathers explain:

Father: It is all about risk management. At the end of the day, I think the environment if I can give it a sort of umbrella, was a lot more user friendly maybe 20 years ago than it is now. There is a greater exposure to potential risk for children today than perhaps there was before. You just need therefore to manage that risk a lot more closely ('middle class', commuter village, Cheshire).

Father: The trouble is you see nowadays there's that many things that happen to kids and happens in split second, they be sexually harassed or they be kidnapped or they be murdered, and it only takes a split second. You know what I mean, and the parents are paying for the rest of their lives. Oh yeah if the bloke gets caught he gets sentenced and all this but that child is dead and them two parents who devoted from that, all that night pain the mother's got up with, nine months she's carrying in her stomach. You know what I mean, it's all gone because of that split second. So you do feel, parents do feel that. I mean I've got three kids, I hear stories on television you know what I mean, it really scares me and I think oh that could be me ('working class', Yorkshire).

In contrast to the past, children no longer have much economic value within the household (and in fact are often a financial drain), but they are more valued in personal and emotional terms. Children increasingly anchor parents' identities. They give parents a foothold into the future, and thus Morgan (1996) argues they provide a bridge between individual time, life course time and historical time. As a result, while individualisation may mean that young people have more choices about how to live their lives, it is parents who are being held responsible for them achieving or fulfilling their opportunities and promise (see also Chapter Five). Beck and Beck-Gernsheim (1995: 119) explain: 'loving a child is an asymmetrical arrangement with all the decisions one-sidely on the parents' shoulders and every mistake likely to interfere with the child's chances in life'. As a consequence, Wyness (1994: 194–5) argues that: 'emotional investment in their children becomes so all-encompassing that parents' social and moral identities are bound up with their parenting roles. Parents' identities become understood in terms of their child-rearing capacities.' As a result contemporary parents are more likely to understand their children's safety in terms of their own self-images as parents (a point returned to in Chapter Three). Parents recognise that if their child were to have a dangerous encounter in public space, that not only would they feel responsible and blame themselves but that others would blame them too. In this sense, children are a 'public' face of families, and as such represent one of the many ways that households are woven into wider structures and practices. These mothers explain:

> Mother: I feel sometimes with children who are abducted it's because they've been allowed to do something that I feel I wouldn't let, you know, mine do. Sometimes you hear about four year olds who've been playing miles from the house and you know I can't understand it cause mine are never let out of my sight ('middle class', commuter village, Cheshire).

> Mother: I think when you look into the actual history of what has happened behind the kids that have been abused, you know there's, I mean there's a degree of responsibility that the parents didn't have towards the children that would've avoided some of the tragedies ('middle class', commuter village, Cheshire).

Moreover, the social construction of childhood as a time of innocence and vulnerability (see Chapter One) means that the risks to children in modernity are represented as inherently more serious than those to adults (Scott et al. 1998). As Holt (1975: 222) points out, 'people who believe in the institution of childhood ... see it as a kind of walled garden in which children, being small and weak, are protected from the harshness of the world outside until they become strong and clever enough to cope with it'. The abduction or murder of a child thus also represents a threat to this association of childhood with specialness and freedom from the adult world (see also Chapter One). It is not therefore just individual children who are perceived to be under threat in modern society; the institution of childhood itself is also at risk of violation.

Parents deal with their concerns about their children's safety by drawing upon a range of information about potential dangers and evaluating this knowledge within the context of their own 'communities'. Two of the most important sources of information are the media and personal/vicarious experience of threatening or dangerous experiences.

Children's safety is an issue that is high on the media agenda in Europe and North America (Cahill 1990, Blakely 1994, Katz 1994). Rare cases of the murder of children in the UK have prompted national newspapers to use headlines such as 'Is a Child Ever Safe?'. Likewise, a small number of cases involving children being contacted by paedophiles on the Internet have also sparked widespread alarm about what has been represented as an increasingly worldwide threat to children. In response to what she described as 'unprecedented concerns for children's safety', a Government Minister warned parents to 'be extra vigilante to prevent further tragedies'. In this way, children are commonly constructed as 'vulnerable' in public places, despite the fact that statistically children, like adults, are more at risk at home from people they know. Commenting on the situation in the US, Cahill (1990: 393) writes:

> ... popular concern about children's safety in public places has mushroomed. A series of highly publicised child abductions and murders ... apparently convinced many Americans that children in public places faced a more ominous danger than moral temptation or accidental injury or death. Televised dramas, documentaries, and Congressional hearings helped to foster the impression that there is a virtual army of villainous adults stalking and preying upon children who dared to venture outside the protective fortress of home and school ... It now often seems as if America in the words of Adam Walsh's [a boy who was abducted and murdered] father, John, is 'littered with mutilated, decapitated, raped and strangled children'.

Katz has (1995: 3) labelled such media coverage 'terror talk'. She argues that '[t]errorizing contentions concerning violence against children in the public arena – from abductions and molestations to armed assaults and murders – weigh heavily on the public imagination' (Katz 1995: 3).

Numerous content analysis studies of newspapers and television have shown that the media exaggerate general crimes of violence against individuals because they are easy to obtain, the human-interest angle makes a good story and they are a useful editing device (Smith 1984, Gordon and Heath 1981). By creating stereotypes of killers, in which they are represented in sub-human terms as beasts, fiends, rippers and so on, where the emphasis is on evil and madness, the media both accentuate fear and create a distance between us (normal) and them (monsters) (Cameron and Frazer 1987, Scott and Watson-Brown 1997). This distance is both metaphorical and spatial in that implicitly 'they' are out there in public space, not in our own homes. This reinforces the perception of danger in public space and makes it harder for both children and adults to recognise and speak out about domestic violence and sexual abuse.

Morley (1986: 169) has observed that women watch more local news because they feel 'if there has been a crime (for instance a rape) in their local area, they need to know about it, both for their own sake and their children's sake'. Yet, the media has made us all global villagers. Thanks to satellite television, the Internet and the global press, news and information from all round the world comes into our homes. As such the evidence of this research is that it is not only local crimes which affect perceptions of fear. National, and even international, cases of child murders were used by some of the parents interviewed to justify the spatial restrictions they impose on their children as a result of their anxieties. Whilst most recognised that the media exaggerated their fears by raising their awareness of extreme and rare incidents, parents claimed that given their heightened knowledge of the possible risks to their children, they could not choose to ignore this information and take any chance with their youngsters' lives, however small they recognised these risks to be.

> Mother: You hear so many stories, you know, and read so many things in the papers. And I know the chances are one in probably millions but you still always think you know, it could be yours and you don't want it to happen, you don't want her to disappear. You don't want anything to happen to them even in a small community like this ('working class', rural village, Derbyshire).

> Mother: I think you should be aware of all dangers that might happen anyway, even though they may not be happening here at the moment, you know, you should always be aware of what could happen. If there are things in the paper about you know, things that happen to children I make a point of showing the children even though you know it might not be anywhere near here ('middle class', commuter village, Cheshire).

> Mother: Whether there are more things happen, or whether we're just more aware of them these days with the press and the telly. I think, I think you are more aware of dangers that can happen and so you tend to protect them more ('middle class', commuter village, Cheshire).

However, parental concerns are not based on media perceptions alone. Several of those interviewed recalled frightening or threatening incidents which they, or someone they know, had experienced. Whilst some of these incidents involved the ubiquitous stranger-danger, others involved threatening encounters with local residents. Social contact is a key method through which information about personal crime is circulated, although not all the 'stories' transmitted in this way are based on traceable sources, and rumour can often exaggerate the relationship between 'race' and crimes of violence (Smith 1984). Awareness of local or vicarious incidents is particularly heightened within small 'communities' where information is spread rapidly – often being elaborated en-route – through close-knit social networks. Such conversations not only pass on information but also provide a forum for informal comment and interpretation in which the story can become exaggerated (Valentine 1992). These interviewees recall several incidents.

> Mother: ... I was walking the dog one day down in the meadows which I'd done, you know, quite happily for a long, long time. I had, um, a problem with a guy that appeared from nowhere and I had to get the police and everything. And you suddenly think ... well maybe anybody, you know, if people have cars these days they can travel anywhere. So I suppose it's, the chances are remote, but we err on the cautious side ('middle class', rural village, Derbyshire).

> Mother: Well I'd never let them up the street, play up street anywhere ... cos it's very busy near the back corner in Wheldale or somebody picking them up, you know, stopping, strangers. Even round here because there was one report of a man going round. We had a letter from the school ... there was one fella ... he was

videoing them down the Rec. [a park], the children. He shouldn't have been there and he was videoing them. And when the police went up to the house they found all these pornographic magazines and everything of children ... [Later in the interview she also recalled an incident in the village when she herself was a child.] It did happen, it happened to this girl I knew, somebody followed her and threw her down, It was down at the picnic area down here but she screamed and luckily this couple was in and come to her rescue. And I think – I think – he'd attacked, it was a local man and I think he'd attacked before ('working class', rural village Derbyshire).

Mother: A certain man in particular, well he's, he was supposed to have molested his own nieces. And it was going round the village about him and he was friendly with a boy from Ashton [a neighbouring village] who sexually, er, molested a little girl ... They took the little girl away cos they did some terrible damage to her and that was just – it's just a mile away. They found out at school because she wouldn't sit down ... [After a short discussion of another incident she and her partner evaluate their knowledge of these cases.] ...
Social Father: But you can't always rely on people's information can you? That's the thing.
Mother: No I've said, you know about those, many, it gets blown out of proportion, a neighbour told me, next door, frightened me to death about that one from Ashton.
Social Father: They go from one to the next and ...
Mother: They add a bit don't they?
Social Father: Yeah, add a bit of spice ('working class', rural village, Derbyshire).

The sort of media and vicarious information described above is interpreted and made sense of in local contexts. In different localities parents collectively define amongst themselves what it means to be a 'good' parent in what Dyck (1990: 475) dubs 'moral consensus' groups. For example, media and vicarious information is used, and made sense of, in informal discussions between parents waiting to collect children outside the school or in car pools etc. and helps to frame mutually agreed local parenting practices in relation children's competence, and the spatial restrictions that should be imposed on them (this process is discussed in more detail in Chapter Three on parenting cultures). As such, although parents may share awareness of national and/or international incidents, because information is interpreted within specific local contexts, different geographies of children's safety may emerge (see also Chapter Five). This is evident, for example, in relation to the village of Wheldale.

The Difference that Place Makes

The countryside is popularly imagined to be a safe, carefree place that offers a sense of belonging and an escape from the dangers of the city: a safe place to grow up (Short 1991, Bell 1992). Parents in the rural village of Wheldale mobilised this understanding of the rural idyll in their accounts of the opportunities that they perceive their children to have to enjoy an 'innocent' childhood away from the social stresses and spatial constraints of the city. At the same time, the parents also contested this imagining of the rural idyll, by contradicting popular assumptions about children's safety in the countryside. Drawing on both the media and local incidents, parents argued that their children are vulnerable, both to what are usually considered 'urban problems', such as stranger-dangers, and to rural demons, such as New Age Travellers and gypsies. Paradoxically, they claimed that the distance between the country and the city has shrunk as a product of the growth in the numbers of cars and thus that the village is potentially more exposed to urban dangers (crime, drugs, joy riders); whilst simultaneously they pointed out that, as a result of economic restructuring, the distance between the town and the country has expanded. For example, the closure of the village police station means that the provision of this service has switched from being locally available to being remote. The effect of the coalescence of this time-space compression and time-space expansion is to emphasise parents' perceptions of their own and their children's vulnerability to stranger-dangers in the village. These paradoxical representations of the rural environment are not however, as contradictory as they first appear. Whilst parents are concerned about their children's safety in Wheldale they still consider them to be safer than children growing up in urban areas because they mobilise another ingredient of the 'rural idyll' – 'community' – to maintain their claims about the relative safety of their children in the village.

Aitken (1994: 76) argues that 'homes and families may be viewed as being nested within neighbourhoods and communities' and that 'these can either serve to bolster rearing or conspire to compound family difficulties'. The Wheldale parents argued that 'the community' played an important role in enabling them to manage their children's safety. The social relations which they (both long-term residents and incomers) described reflect what Tonnies (1955) has termed a *gemeinshaft* notion of community. Harper (1989: 62) defines this as 'close human relationships developed through kinship linked to place through a common habitat, and sharing co-operation and co-ordinate action for a common good' – to describe the social relations in the village. These claims of an ethos of co-operation and mutual aid have characterised numerous previous studies of rural life (Bell 1992, Little and Austin 1996).

The community is not 'real' in the sense that everybody literally knows everybody else, nor is it 'real' in the sense that they all necessarily get on. Rather, there are many complex social relations between different groups of adults and children in the village (particularly a tension between long-term residents and newcomers). However, despite these multiple processes of 'sameness' and 'othering', parents still mobilised an illusion of an 'imagined community' (Anderson 1983) to justify their claim that they can manage their children's safety more easily and successfully in Wheldale than if they lived in an urban environment.

Specifically, the parents of Wheldale argued the social networks in the village ensure that their children are safer than those who live in, what they claim, are the more anonymous worlds of the town or the city. They feel confident that there are always 'eyes on the street' (Jacobs 1961) to keep their children under observation. Indeed some argued that the gaze of nosy neighbours could be rather too intrusive. The sense of 'family' and small scale nature of the village primary school also encouraged the parents to feel confident that their children were safe both in, and coming out of, school, because the teachers and other parents would notice and would intervene if there was a stranger at the school gates or if a parent had not arrived to collect their child.

Mother: I would hate to live probably anywhere bigger than Wheldale … I think it is probably safer in that everybody knows Sarah. There are a lot of people in the village who know Sarah in fact, more people know Sarah than know me and I think that helps to make it safer for her. Maybe in towns and cities they don't get to know people quite so well ('working class', rural village, Derbyshire).

Mother: There is an awareness that people know who each other are and as soon as there's someone there that's not right, we're all asking who they are. Because with it being a small village you do know each other. I think in bigger towns you haven't got a clue who each other are. So I mean that is an extra precaution that at least if your child is seen with someone you know whether it's someone local or not ('middle class', rural village, Derbyshire).

Mother: I mean I think it's like in a village everybody knows everybody don't they and if they see kids walking home and anything went wrong I think they would intervene, you know. Like in a city probably people wouldn't do the same because they wouldn't know them would they? ('working class', rural village, Derbyshire).

In this way then, it is evident that while parents may share national or even global fears about issues such as children's safety, these concerns are not played out the same everywhere. Rather, they are interpreted and made sense of within local contexts producing subtly different geographies of parental fear.

Educating Children about Danger

There is a tension for parents in wanting to prioritise time-future by keeping their children safe, while at the same time giving them a time-present by allowing them the freedom to play (Kelley et al. 1997). Moreover, time-present is important in teaching children the skills and independence they need to become competent adults of the future. One of the ways that parents try to balance their perception of children as at risk from stranger-dangers, while also trying to develop their skills to manage and take risks for themselves, is through educating them about personal safety (and also institutional play, see Chapter Five).

However, despite the fact that children are statistically more likely to be abused in 'private space' by a person known to them than in public space, and that many children experience the home as a place of domestic conflict, strife and parental pressure (NSPCC 2000), the crude dichotomy of public-danger versus the safety of the home is fed to many young people through the combined agencies of parents, schools, the police, media and private educational programmes.

One reason for the reproduction of this misleading message about the geography of danger, is the reluctance of many schools to allow the police to talk to children about forms of violence that may occur in private space. It is argued that children should learn about sexuality within the 'privacy' of the 'family', and that educating them about inappropriate touch may confuse them about the 'innocent' moments that many parents share with their youngsters at home and undermine children's trust in loving adults. At the same time mothers and fathers are often reluctant to address these issues with their children believing that the classroom is the best place for children to learn about sex (Wyness 1997) because teachers will know when to tell children the 'right' things at the most appropriate time (Jackson and Scott 1999). Yet, teachers are equally uncomfortable about providing sex education because it puts them in the 'moral firing line' (Wyness 2000: 120). Moreover, it is easy for children to embarrass teachers by making links between the general and the personal, so threatening teachers' identities and authority (Wyness 2000).

Given this general adult squeamishness about talking to the young about sexuality and the body, rather than deal with the complexities of children's vulnerability it is easier for schools and parents to paint a broad picture of the 'stranger' in the street who kidnaps children. This robs the message about danger of any sexual content, thereby pulling off the paradoxical feat of warning youngsters about sexual violence whilst apparently protecting childhood innocence (Valentine 1996a). Although this is a concern that is in many cases misplaced given the amount of sexual information available to children in different media (Jackson 1996, Holloway and Valentine 2003) and the fact that children often first learn about sex from peers in the playground. As a result Scott et al. (1998: 700) argue that 'children have to struggle to make sense of a jigsaw puzzle of knowledge from which many pieces are missing'. This police officer and a mother describe how they deal with talking to children about stranger-dangers:

Police Officer: I would find it very difficult to say to a child you're going to be sexually assaulted and that sort of thing [laughs uncomfortably]. So I don't. I just say don't go with strangers and they believe this mystic about it, that it is going to be the most horrid thing that will ever happen to you if you go with them, and leave them with that bit of fear ... When I come into this job I was very, very enthusiastic

... I was going to go on about like inappropriate touching. But er no you can't say that. You can't like any, like any sexual anything that could be construed as being as a sexual nature they wouldn't allow in the school ... How do we, how do you then say that sort of thing because being a parent you touch your child and that sort of thing and so do they then say if Mum or Dad touches me there is that inappropriate touching or affection. So that was one of the concerns that I had and I didn't ... I thought I'm not going to, I'm not going to entertain it.

Mother: I think that its very difficult for a child to handle, you know. I mean we don't want them to be terrified ... it's a difficult one. I have said that there are some men who like to do things to little children ... I think that's as much as they can cope with, you know you don't want to go into graphic details ... I don't think you have to know the mechanics of it. But it's I mean I think you know we do always warn them about going off with strange people, even though the tragedy of it, it's very often people that they know ('middle class', commuter village, Cheshire).

By reproducing a misleading message about the geography of danger stranger-danger educational campaigns contribute towards producing public space as 'naturally' or 'normally' an adult space where children are at risk from 'deviant' others. A space in which the male body in particular is saturated with threat and danger. But whilst the male body is constituted through fear, the female body is marked as safe. It is women, particularly those with children, that youngsters are taught to turn to in the face of danger. This father and two police officers describe the advice they give:

Father: I always say, especially to my little girl, now listen darling if you see anybody you don't recognise darling, if he wants to talk to you don't say nothing to him, just cross the road and just come, make your way home. If he's pestering you and there's a lot of women around just tell somebody 'he won't leave me alone', then they'll go away, you know what I mean ('working class', metropolitan area, Yorkshire).

Police Officer: I'll try to establish what, what is a stranger. I always say it's somebody that you don't know. Just trying to keep it simple so the little ones understand. I always use the yell, run and tell thing which the kids can remember. The people who we say are safe to go to are lady shop assistants and a lady with children is safe person to go to. I say to them all about this strangers and things like that but I always say to them at the end and I try to stress to them that 'I don't want you to be frightened, you know, to go to sleep tonight because you think some man's gonna come in and grab you and that'.

Police Officer: You can do it in various ways. There is a video that you take out – obviously the video now might be getting a bit old, but it, it sort of, it shows you at different stages – you know the chap in the car with the sweets waits at the school for the child whose parents haven't turned up. There's the other one where there's a boy and a girl at a park, the lad wants to do something better and leaves the girl and obviously someone comes and is walking her away when obviously her parents and whatever come and see all this happening and the bloke disappears.

This marking of the male body means that many fathers now feel unable to interact with children in public places through a fear of being mistaken as a 'dangerous stranger'. Whereas on crowded public transport and in supermarket checkout queues, men could once treat children as a temporary source of amusement by smiling, pulling faces at them or engaging them in conversation, men claim that now they feel that their behaviour and even sometimes their presence is read as threatening as these quotes demonstrate:

Mother: I'd seen her [a female friend, Brenda] and she'd said this old man had sort of said hello to Julia the youngest child. And Julia didn't know this man and she'd ignored him and the chap apparently turned round to Brenda and said what a rude little girl she was ... You instil into children don't talk to strangers so of course she ignored this old man who was probably quite, it was all innocent, but he was saying 'hello little girl' that sort of thing and she totally ignored him because she'd been taught never to talk to strangers ('middle class', non-metropolitan area, Derbyshire).

Mother: He [her husband] was going down the street and a little girl was I don't know cycling a bike or something um and her mother had got another toddler and the little girl fell off the bike. He went to get the girl up and make sure she was alright and the mother sort of verbally attacked him, 'Keep away from my child, what do you think you're doing?' ('middle class', rural area, Cheshire).

Father: We went to this show ... and this little kiddie comes wandering up ... and he's crying 'where's my Mummy?' And my immediate reaction was God, you know, keep the kid here where he's safe, don't let him go wandering round, but at the same time it was God, I hope nobody thinks I'm taking this kid. And I was terrified to actually hold on to the child in case somebody thought I was taking him ('middle class', rural area, Cheshire).

Through this demonisation of the male body children are being encouraged to trust no one (or no man) and to be on their guard against the most casual of encounters in the most anodyne of places, becoming early experts at manoeuvring out of others' way, minimising expressivity and conveying disinterest. There is also a danger of producing a message in which children are presented as victims rather than highlighting the resistances that they might be able to put up.

By withdrawing from interactions with adults, particularly men in public space, children contribute towards producing public space as an adult space where they are not able to participate freely. As David Sibley (1995a: 16) points out: 'For children in the most highly developed societies, the house is becoming increasingly a haven ... At the same time, the outside becomes more threatening, populated by potential molesters and abductors so the boundary between the home (safe) and the locality (threatening) is more strongly defined.' The flip side of this is also that children are not made aware of the possibility that the family home might also be a site of abuse (Kitzinger

1990, NSPCC 2000). For this reason the UK children's charity Kidscape's 'Keeping Safe' material encourages children to challenge all forms of inappropriate touching and to take responsibility for their own bodies.

By contributing to the production of public space as an adult space the stranger-danger message has some advantages for adults. As Qvortrup (1994: 21) observes, 'there is … an inherent risk of exaggerating it [the need to protect children] and to the extent this happens it may turn into its opposite, namely a convenient tool to protect the adult world against the intrusion of children'. In particular, the production of public space as too dangerous for children to negotiate independently, can serve adults' control and ownership of young people so that, for example, the stranger-danger warning is often mobilised by parents as a catchall threat to keep children off the streets and therefore away from drugs, under age sex or mixing with the 'wrong' crowd (a point returned to in Chapter Five). In this way, some adults can stifle children's competence and keep them dependent, so ignoring their ability to manage their own lives, overriding their independent use of space and protestations that they will not get into trouble or can look after themselves[2] (Waksler 1986). As Waksler (1986: 78) argues, '[a]dults and children have separate versions of childhood. Adulthood is a perspective, a way of being in the world, that embodies a particular stance towards children, a stance that allows adults to "deal with" children in everyday life'.

In summary, this chapter has focused on the ways that parental fears for children's safety in public space are constructed and mobilised through the media, vicarious experiences, 'community' and educational campaigns. In particular, it has looked at terror talk and risk assessment, to suggest that global and national reporting of violent crimes against children may distort local fears by heightening parents' awareness of extreme and rare events in public space causing them to restrict their children's use of space excessively, while also obscuring the extent to which children are at risk in 'private' space and from people they know. This false geography of fear potentially makes it more difficult for children to recognise or speak up about unsafe experiences in domestic contexts.

At the same time, however, the chapter has also shown how the stories that circulate about dangers to children are interpreted and made sense of within different local 'communities' and has drawn attention to the way that 'community' might mediate fears (see also Chapter Seven), and also to the extent to which terror talk demonises men in public space. The following chapter develops these themes further by examining how parental fears are (re)produced and negotiated within the context of local parenting cultures, and the way that both parents' fears for children's safety, and the culture and conduct of parenting, are gendered.

Notes

1   This question allowed for more than one response.
2   Paradoxically, however, the marking of male bodies as 'dangerous' which means that many men (and some women) no longer feel free to engage with unknown children in everyday spaces means that youngsters actually have greater freedom from unwanted adult interventions and hence more privacy in public space. In this way, the street is simultaneously constituted through fear as a space where children are vulnerable to adults but also as a space where they have limited autonomy from adults.

Chapter 3

Gender and Parenting Cultures

The dominant twentieth century western society imagining of children as vulnerable, incompetent and in need of protection – that was outlined in Chapter One – contributes towards structuring the way we think about parenting and how children should be brought up. Popular discourses about appropriate ways to raise children are produced around many different issues, from what they should be fed or clothed in, to what they should be allowed to watch on television. As the previous chapter outlined, recent high profile cases of child abductions and murders in both the US and UK have focused attention on parenting cultures and children's safety in public space. Parents determine the extent of their children's personal geographies by deciding at what age they should be allowed outside alone and at what age and when, they may go to different places (the shops, school, the park, the city centre etc.) unaccompanied by an adult. This chapter begins by considering whether, and how, parents vary these sorts of boundaries according to the gender, age and position in the family of their children. It then goes on to consider how what it means to be a 'good parent' – in terms of managing children's independent use of space – is negotiated and contested within different local communities.

The process of managing children's safety within individual households is highly gendered in terms of how mothers and fathers negotiate the parental responsibilities of setting children's spatial boundaries and discipline any infringements. The final sections of this chapter therefore focus on the culture and conduct of both motherhood and fatherhood. Consideration is also given to the ways that parenting decisions, and the gendered division of childcare are further complicated by the diverse, fluid and complex nature of many contemporary families (see also Chapter One). In particular, the chapter reflects on the way that mothers' and fathers' roles and responsibilities are negotiated and contested between 'biological' and 'social' parents in lone parent and reconstituted families.

Gender and Home Range

Previous research has identified gender and age variations in the sort of restrictions that parents place on their children's use of public space in order to keep them safe (Ward 1978, Hart 1979, Matthews 1987). Unsurprisingly, as children get older they are usually allowed to range further from home by their parents. For example, a study of children in an anonymous US town identified a significant leap in children's spatial ranges (the distance children travel away from home unaccompanied by an adult) at the age of ten (Hart 1979). This is the age at which their parents regarded them to be competent to deal with traffic. Both this and other studies (van Vliet 1983, Bjorklid 1985, Katz 1993) have found that boys are usually allowed to range further from home unsupervised and to spend more time outdoors than girls. This gender difference in children's geographies has been explained in terms of parents' greater concern for daughters' safety and the fact that girls' activities are more constrained because they have more responsibilities in the home than boys (Hart 1979). In this way, it is argued that discourses about women's sexual vulnerability in 'public' space' (Valentine 1989) and a woman's 'place' in the home shape not only adults', but also girls' use of space (Saegert and Hart 1978).

However, the evidence of this research suggests that parents may be holding more complex and contradictory views about gender and safety than previous studies have implied (Valentine 1997a). While some parents maintained a 'traditional' view that girls are both more vulnerable to sexual attack and less able to defend themselves than boys, others argued that they are equally concerned about the vulnerability of their sons and daughters in public space. For example, 51 per cent of the parents responding to the questionnaire survey said that they considered all children to be equally at risk of abduction. Statistical analysis of the questionnaire results also revealed no significant relationships between the sex of a parents' child and their concerns about safety, the places which they ranked as the most dangerous for their child or the way that their child travels to school. Indeed, 34 per cent of the responses from parents with daughters indicated that they considered their girls to be most at risk in the road outside the home, compared with 32 per cent of the responses from parents with sons.

These results support the findings of recent sociological research on parenting that has suggested that expectations about sex-typed behaviours are changing both within, and outside, the family. Likewise, studies of children's play, have found commonalities between girls and boys play, but also complex variations between, and within, these groups (Thorne 1994). Some of the different views about gender and children's safety offered by interviewees in this study are reflected in these quotes:

> Father: My concerns don't differ much now. I could see they would do in a few years to come. At the moment the age they are they've got the same – they've got the traffic problem, they've got abduction, child molesters and child killers, which is, it doesn't matter whether they're male or female with children they [molesters] don't seem to bother. When, in another six or seven years my concerns will be different. Here's a lot of violence on older children when they're out. So I would be more concerned about my son then the way things are going. There's less chance of violence and bullying with a girl than there is with a lad ('working class', urban metropolitan borough, Greater Manchester).

Mother: I really don't think girls are more at risk of being sexually abused than boys, it happens to lads as well unfortunately, but I think boys are also more prone to physical violence than girls or getting in with the wrong crowd ('middle class', urban non-metropolitan borough, Cheshire).

The high profile given to a number of cases involving the abduction and sexual murder of boys led many parents to claim that up to the age of puberty boys are equally as vulnerable as girls to sexually motivated assaults. However, whereas previous research has argued that after puberty parents become more confident in the physical ability of boys to defend themselves against abductors and, therefore, their concerns for their sons' safety diminishes, these findings suggest that rather than evaporating post puberty parents' fears for their sons merely take on a different form. Whilst parents perceive teenage girls to be vulnerable to sexual assault, they perceive teenage boys to be vulnerable to random male violence at football grounds, pubs and on the streets. In this respect their fears are consistent with statistics which suggest that the group most at risk from interpersonal violence are young men (Stanko 1987). Concerns for teenage boys' safety were particularly evident amongst south Asian parents in Yorkshire, who were concerned that their sons' vulnerability to racially motivated violence will increase rather than dissipate as they grow up; and amongst parents from a 'middle class' urban metropolitan borough in Greater Manchester where the questionnaires and interviews revealed a local problem with gangs.

Mother: I worry about, I must admit I worry about racist attacks, right and – Retan, the old, the oldest one … I worry about the racist attacks, I worry about him going up to the senior school right because I'm not sure how he'll be able to handle it … As a male growing up, I think things are so violent for them … it's a lot harder for them as they're growing up, it's so violent, you know, they, whether they want to or not, they've got to be involved in that ('working class', urban metropolitan area, Yorkshire).

Parental views about boys' and girls' differential abilities to protect themselves in public space also appear to be shifting. Parents stress the need for children to develop common sense before they can successfully negotiate public space alone (Wyness 1994). It is girls aged 8–11 who tend to be regarded as more responsible, more rational and to have more self control than boys. This is a rather ironic reversal of the historical construction of women as hysterical and men as rational and logical beings (Nesmith and Radcliffe 1993). As a consequent parents perceive their daughters to be less vulnerable in public places than their sons because the girls are perceived to have the nous to anticipate danger and to take appropriate action to avoid or cope with a dangerous or threatening situation. Boys of this age, in contrast, were portrayed as immature and irrational and consequently as unable to take responsibility for negotiating public space safely. Those in 'working class' rather than 'middle class' areas, were also described as more easily led by peers than girls. This lack of self awareness amongst boys in public space was related in turn to parents' perceptions of gender differences in sexual maturity. Mothers argued that their daughters were very aware of their bodies and sexuality at an early age. Whereas mothers were able to address issues of sex and sexuality and emotions with their daughters (particularly at puberty), parents found it harder to initiate these conversations with their sons and were concerned that their sons were consequently more vulnerable to 'inappropriate touch' because of their 'innocence'. Girls were also credited with having more verbal skills than boys and therefore more ability to deal with any potentially dangerous encounters. These anecdotal representations of gender traits correlate with other research that suggests that boys are more difficult to raise; develop more slowly emotionally and physically; and are more disobedient and likely to get into trouble than girls (Downey et al. 1994). These parents describe the differences that they observe between boys and girls:

> Mother: She's very aware of people, whereas he isn't. He'll talk to anybody, anybody at all, he'll speak to, I think I have to be more protective of him because he's that way, whereas she's different, you know, she's more of a stronger person ('working class', rural town, Derbyshire).

> Mother: I think I protect him more because he's the sort of person who would go with somebody, you know, because he's so trusting. I mean she's got enough sense, but I mean the other day he came in and I says 'oh, where've you been', and he says 'he let me sit on it [a neighbour allowed him to sit on a motorbike] and he gave me loads of stickers'. Now as it happens the bloke he's on about is a policeman but he didn't know that, he could have been anybody, you know and I mean all he'd got to say is 'Do you want to sit on my motorbike?', so it just proves that it doesn't matter how much you tell 'em they still go at the first opportunity ('middle class', urban non-metropolitan borough, Cheshire).

> Mother: My son's a bit dizzy [laughter]. He is, he's sometimes not, sometimes he's on another planet, you know, he, he, he's not very responsible at all really, he's [pause] I mean you do say to him 'Don't get into strangers' cars or whatever' but I could see him doing it, I could. She's more level headed. She would come 'No', it would come straightaway. She's more sensible. She's quite a dominant person ... she can take care of herself [laughter] ('middle class', rural village, Derbyshire).

> Father: The little'un, Ghazala, she's just in a class of her own. I can't compare her with anybody ... she's, she's the strongest out of the three of 'em, she's right strong personality. Mentally as well she's, she's the one that's most aware. Very you know, what do you call it, detailed eye, if something's out of place or something's wrong ('working class', urban metropolitan area, Yorkshire).

Parents were not always in agreement about the relative vulnerability of their offspring. Whilst some fathers adopted the more 'traditional' line that girls are the gender most at risk, mothers were more likely to contradict them and point out their daughters' personal characteristics.

> Mother: I think it's equal [boys are as much as risk as girls] I know you [to husband] worry about girls because you think they are delicate and feminine but Sarah isn't. On the whole people tend to think of girls as being defenceless but actually boys tend to be more insecure than girls. I think girls are much more self possessed at an earlier age than boys are. I think Sarah, you know anybody who tries to handle her is in trouble ('middle class', rural village, Derbyshire).
> Father: I suppose being a Dad yeah you're going to say you're going to worry more for your daughter than your son – but yeah I think so. You tend to think that you know your son is able to look after himself better, maybe that's a bit sexist. I don't know, but that's the way you feel.
> Mother: I think I worry for them both the same ('middle class', urban non-metropolitan borough, Cheshire).

Not all parents however, assessed their children's competence to deal with strangers on the basis of assumptions (traditional or otherwise) about their gender. Rather, they acknowledged the importance of their children's individual personalities, recognising that these do not always tally with gendered expectations. In particular, parents appear to adopt a fluid approach to the meanings and responsibilities ascribed to their children's 'age', sometimes simultaneously defining their child's age in contradictory ways (Solberg 1990). For example, one parent pointed out, that whilst she places very extreme limitations on her son's use of public space, she does allow him a wide range of responsibilities in the home. In contrast, her sister's children are given more leeway to play outside unsupervised but are not allowed to do simple domestic tasks, such as make toast. This notion of 'competence' is discussed in more detail in Chapter Four.

Whilst parents' constructions of the age at which individual children can negotiate public space alone safely may wax and wane according to the child's ability to consistently demonstrate maturity, there does appear to be a watershed age, 11–12, at which all parents accept that their children will be given greater licence to negotiate public space alone. This is the age at which children normally progress from a primary school to a senior school, necessitating a longer journey (often by public transport) to school and a change in peer group and associated activities, all of which require or encourage children to take on more responsibility for themselves and to seek greater independence from their parent(s).

Position in the Family

'Evidence from oral history and childhood autobiography shows that in the past, children, especially girls, helped at home by looking after younger siblings to a significant extent, particularly in working class families' (Morrow 1994: 134). But just as parents' sex-based expectations are changing, so too it appears that expectations in relation to place in the family are being reconceptualised.

Hart's (1979) research on children's experience of place found that older girls were often given responsibility for younger siblings in public places (consistent with other cross-cultural studies, for example, Bigner 1974). This limited the spatial range of older girls but enabled younger children in the company of 'Big Sister' to enjoy more extended spatial ranges than 'first born' children. Indeed, having older siblings gives children more structural support to do things with others independently of parents (Lamb and Sutton-Smith 1982). Brim (1958) also suggests that children with opposite sex siblings demonstrate more characteristics of the opposite sex than children whose siblings are the same sex because it is easier for parents to maintain polarised attitudes about girls and boys if they only have children of the same sex. Following this logic, boys with sisters should be more protected than those with brothers, whilst girls with brothers should have greater freedom than those with only sisters as siblings.

However, this study suggests that position in the family has only a minor effect on parents' attitudes towards children's safety and the level of restrictions that they impose on their offspring's use of space. 'Middle class' parents argued that as children they had to watch over younger siblings but that they do not believe that it is fair to place this burden of responsibility on their own older children (although this appeared to be a more acceptable practice amongst 'working class' and south Asian parents). This is because brothers and sisters have relationships with each other that are independent of their relationships with parents, which means that a younger child may not necessarily respect or obey an older child. Moreover, these parents were also concerned that an older child may not look after younger ones in the same way that an adult would (indeed there is a general anxiety about whether anyone else can be trusted to watch over children as closely as parents themselves do). In other words, an older daughter is more like her younger brother than she is like her parents. Finally, parents felt they had to be more protective of their own children than their parents had been of them when they were young because children are perceived to be more at risk today (see also Chapters Two and Five).

These arguments for treating children as individuals rather than as carers for each other reflect both the seriousness with which parents' regard the dangers children may encounter in public space, and the extent to which middle class parents regard childhood as a time when children should be free from all the responsibilities (such as looking after others) of adulthood (as outlined in Chapter One). These parents explain their views on sibling carers:

> Mother: I mean I can remember going down to the park when I was a child but I always had my older brothers and sisters with me. So I mean I did go to the park without my parents but I had older children with me, more responsible children. But I would never expect, there's no way I'd expect Katie to take Michael to the park, so he doesn't go ('middle class', urban non-metropolitan borough, Cheshire).

> Mother: I'm the youngest girl me, well the youngest girl of six but there's two lads younger than me. The middle girl always had to have me tagging on and I always stressed I wouldn't ever do that to mine and I never have, you know, they've got separate lives and separate friends ('middle class', urban metropolitan borough, Greater Manchester).

> Mother: I can't really expect Natalie to be responsible for Mark because if he's got something in his head he doesn't want to do and she knows its wrong, he'll do it anyway, you know, whatever she says ('middle class', rural village, Derbyshire).

Having older siblings does however appear to mean that children win their independence slightly earlier than first born or only children. This is because older children demonstrate their competence to negotiate public space safely (see Chapter Four) and so gradually wear down parents' resistance to, and arguments against, younger siblings requests for greater freedoms. There does not, however, appear to be any significant differences in the opportunities for independence accorded to children according to the gender of their siblings. If anything female siblings appear to increase the independent opportunities for male siblings because of their perceived greater maturity, rather than the other way round.

> Father: We have always given, each one has had a little bit more freedom than the last one. We were quite strict on the oldest girl and slowly the two years apart have been a little more lenient but usually they [parents] are with the older one ('middle class', urban non-metropolitan borough, Cheshire).

Whilst parents attitudes towards their offspring are often (though not always) highly gendered (traditionally or otherwise), so too, are cultures of parenting and parenting practices. Children's safety, because it is about the control of children's bodies and their space, is one domestic issue where tensions between mothers and fathers, and between 'biological' and 'social' parents are often exposed. The following two sections address the culture and conduct of motherhood and of fatherhood respectively.

The Culture and Conduct of Motherhood

'At least since the nineteenth century, motherhood has been glorified as women's chief vocation and central definition. The tie between mother and child has been exalted, and traits of nurturance, selflessness, and altruism have been defined as the essence of the maternal, and hence, the womanly' (Thorne 1982: 11). Indeed, in the nineteenth century, because motherhood was one of the few activities that gave women any status and power in the household, campaigns for women's rights, were often couched in terms of the need for more respect for mothers rather than challenging gender divisions of childcare (Gordon 1982).

This attitude to motherhood changed at the turn of the twentieth century when new reproductive technologies (specifically birth control), the fall in the economic value of children and new lifestyle aspirations led to a drop in the birth rate (starting in middle class families). Gordon (1982: 47) explains:

> By the early twentieth century the further development of industrial capitalism had begun to allow a vision of greater independence for women. Not only prosperous women but also working-class women in the World War I era were experiencing the effects of public education, mass employment of women, the transformation of virtually the entire male population into a wage labour force and extensive commodity production replacing most household production.

As a result of the devaluing of domestic work (including motherhood) and the increase in opportunities for women to participate in public life, feminist attitudes to motherhood and birth control changed with a new emphasis being placed on the restrictions bearing exclusive responsibility for childcare/ family imposed on women's lives. Contemporary feminism has further challenged the culture of motherhood (the social construction of mothering), attempting both to demystify it by publicising women's diverse experiences of mothering (for example, post-natal depression, isolation, stress, loss of individuality) and to represent it as a choice (for example, by supporting birth control, abortion, lesbian rights to motherhood) rather than as a positive and essential experience for all women (e.g. Phoenix and Woollett 1991, Boulton 1983, Chodorow and Contratto 1982). At the same time it has also sought to facilitate the conduct of motherhood (what mothers actually do) by promoting equal rights for mothers in the labour market, and work-based childcare.

Whilst the romanticization of motherhood has been challenged by women's diverse accounts of the meanings of motherhood, the conduct of motherhood has also become more diverse at the end of the twentieth century. Economic restructuring, the decline in manufacturing jobs and consequent feminization of the labour force mean that many women are not secondary wage earners within households, but the primary earners (Stacey 1990). This combined with the growth in lone parent families and consequent feminization of childhood (Jensen 1994) mean that fathers and other carers are viewed as marginally significant in an increasing number of children's lives.[1]

Despite these changes in the conduct of motherhood, the dominant contemporary cultural understandings of motherhood still simultaneously idealise mothers (as the guardians of children's welfare) and blame them if their children do not 'turn out right'. Mothers are constructed as responsible for the preservation (from the moment of conception onwards), growth (physical, emotional and intellectual) and social acceptability of their children (Ruddick 1982). Bowlby (1969), for example, placed an emphasis on the isolation of mother and child, arguing that the intimate and continuous relationship between a mother and child is essential for normal emotional development. These, largely white middle class, constructions of motherhood have been professionalised by medical and childcare manuals, producing very limited definitions of appropriate ways that children should be reared. Mothers should not, for example, be very young (under 20), very old (over 40), lesbian, or lone parents. Those who are perceived or assumed to deviate from white, middle class 'norms' are frequently accused of producing unruly or deviant children (see also Chapter Six) (Phoenix and Woollett 1991, Chodorow and Contratto 1982). Moral panics about the state of 'the nuclear family' and contemporary childhood are also commonly accompanied by demands that women should stay at home with their offspring.

This mismatch between the culture (romanticised ideal that mothers are powerful and should be perfect) and conduct of contemporary motherhood (many mothers are in paid employment and are bringing their children up in postmodern rather than traditional nuclear families) means that despite the lack of any evidence to justify the accusations of 'inadequacy' levelled against contemporary mothers (Walkerdine and Lucey 1989), many women feel guilty for not living up to the ideal representations of motherhood, while they still do the lion's share of childcare work (Brannen and Moss 1988).

The evidence of this research is that mothers spend more time with children and bear more of the burden and responsibilities of keeping them safe during the day than fathers. Women, for example, are more likely than men to work part time, job share or use flexi time to be with their children (Grimm-Thomas and Perry-Jenkins 1994). Whereas men do most of their 'family' work at weekends, women do it all the time. It is usually mothers therefore who are most aware of how competent or incompetent their children are at negotiating public space and who establish day-to-day boundaries (see also Chapter Four). This mother explains:

Mother: I think Alan tends to be a bit more protective because he is, he's not with them as often, so he may be not aware of, you know, what they're capable of doing, you know, what they're sensible enough to do … Alan works quite long hours so he's not always there to, you know if they ask something, you know to do something different, … so I think I decide more ('middle class', commuter village, Cheshire).

Rather than trying to supervise their children's outdoor play in order to keep them safe, parents are increasingly encouraging children to spend their time either in the home with friends or taking part in activities organised by adults (such as music lessons, sports training and so on) in order to have more control over their safety (see also Chapter Five). It is largely (though not exclusively) mothers, however, who bear the daily burden of ferrying children to and from home, school and these activities – journeys which imposes severe constraints on women's own activities. Indeed, Dowling (2000) argues that the car has become crucial to 'good mothering'. Although ironically, in trying to protect their own children by taking them in the car, mothers increase the volume of traffic on the roads and so put other children at risk. These mothers describe their roles:

> Mother: It's very very restricting ... This is why I'm not working at the moment, well why I'm working nights, because between school holidays and her still being at the age where she isn't quite yet old enough to go to and from school ... the young 'un isn't old enough yet to have a key and come home herself, you know so I'm pretty restricted in a lot of ways ('working class', urban metropolitan borough, Greater Manchester).

> Mother: I have to go to Pyms Road to pick Mark up, come back and then go back and then go back again to pick Natalie up and it's a five mile trip, well its a ten mile round trip you know. Like tonight I've been down twice. I went down to pick up Mark up at half three, quarter past three and Natalie stayed behind for pantomime so then I've been down to pick her up at quarter to five ... It's very time consuming, like I leave at twenty-five past eight to take them to school on a morning and then I'm back again about ten past nine but then I go out again about ten to three for Natalie then we'll drive round for Mark and then we're back here about twenty to four but then they've always got something after school so I'm back again ('middle class', urban non-metropolitan, Cheshire).

Taking the primary role for managing children's use of space and time means that mothers are also the first to come under pressure from their youngsters to extent their spatial ranges. There is often a different bond between mothers and their children than between fathers and their children. Whilst youngsters often perceive their mothers to be more responsive and sympathetic than fathers; fathers are commonly described as more powerful and autocratic (Thompson and Walker 1989). Certainly, mothers appear to be more flexible and willing to accept children's reasoning or accounts of why their range should be extended and they also witness at first hand the peer group pressure that their offspring come under. Paradoxically therefore, whilst mothers were often presented as the gender most anxious and 'fussy' about their children's safety, they were also identified as the 'softest' parent (a point children exploit, see Chapter Four). Often under domestic and emotional pressure, they give in to their children's requests to be allowed out (further and longer), and therefore appear to be less consistent than fathers in their parenting practices. In contrast, because fathers are often more distanced from their children's daily lives it appears to be easier for them to maintain ideal boundaries and rules. They do not have to deal, for example, with seeing their children cry because all their friends have been allowed to go somewhere that they have been forbidden to go. Rather it is mothers who often experience the tension of, on the one hand being emotionally close and sympathetic to their children, and on the other hand, the pressure to be authoritarian and consistently uphold the spatial boundaries agreed with, or set by, a partner.

Although taking prime responsibility for children is a major constraint on women's lives that can undermine their own sense of self, motherhood can also give women a sense of meaning and identity (Thompson and Walker 1989). Children have the power to affect the status and social esteem of their parents, (particularly mothers), because parents, (particularly mothers), are responsible for them (Harris 1983, Hood Williams 1990). Isabel Dyck (1989a, 1989b, 1990) has argued that routine practices of mothering and what it means to be a 'good' mother are constructed and contested locally, and that social interactions between mothers plays an important part in this process. She argues that discussions and interpretations of how children should be looked after and the transmission of this 'expertise' take place both in structured settings, such as at car pools, children's sports clubs, volunteer organisations and institutions and through professional discourses, including the media (Dyck 1990). She (Dyck 1989a: 335) states that '[t]he sharing of information and discovery of rules neighbours use to govern their children's activity is an important part of how women manage their children's relationship to the proximate social and physical environment'.

Many of the mothers interviewed were conscious of the pressures on them to live up to the ideal of what was constructed as 'good' practice and were anxious to avoid the blame (for being too lax or too strict) and the guilt that goes with failing to keep in line with peer 'moral consensus' groups. 'Middle class' mothers appeared to be more protective than those from low income families and stressed the obligations on them to impose common restrictions on their children's spatial ranges and to chaperone their children to and from activities as these women explain:

Mother: I mean we all get together, we all – I think we all do the same and I think sometimes when we hear that some parents have allowed their children to go various places, you know, eyebrows are raised ('middle class', commuter village, Cheshire).

Mother: You think 'cos I'll say it sometimes to Gemma [friend], I say well I said is David allowed to do that or er is Simon allowed or ? And you think umm … it's a difficult one you're always checking yourself against other people I think to see what is the norm ('middle class', urban metropolitan borough, Greater Manchester).

Mother: I mean a lot of Mums [pause] it sounds a bit, a bit cliquey really, but they seem to segregate themselves at school, you know what I mean? You get a lot of

Mums they all live together on the Baddow estate and they all stand together and chat together and maybe they do let their kids roam all over the place and then there's the other Mums that don't let their kids wander all over the place and know exactly, I mean I know where mine are 24 hours a day but there's a lot of Mums that don't ('middle class', urban non-metropolitan area, Cheshire).

Mother: If I don't go to school to pick the children up I feel very, very guilty because all the Mums are there. I wouldn't not pick her up. I think Laura's quite old enough to really walk home from school on her own but guilt makes you go [to collect her] because it's expected [by the other mums] ('middle class', commuter village, Cheshire).

South Asian mothers particularly emphasised the importance of strong local 'family' and 'community' networks in their childcare arrangements. These both facilitate women's ability to look after their children by enabling them to share the burden of childcare with friends and neighbours but also serve as a pressure on them to maintain certain boundaries and parenting practices.

Mother: You see, with us, with our family, the kids are with us all the time, you know, we don't let them, you know if they're gonna play they usually play with us ... I know people think it's wrong but this is our society you know, the way we were brought up together, we can't hide anything from each other, everything is open in the family, you know what I mean' (translation, 'working class', urban metropolitan area Yorkshire).

Father: It's close knit [the local south Asian community] and although we're from different areas of Kashmir and Pakistan on the road, we've, I've actually grown up with the parents that're now parents, like when we weren't married, when we were kids we played in the street ... so there is, there tends to be like a family network, there's security ... there's not always community harmony but if there's a problem then we'll stick together to sort it out ('working class', urban metropolitan area, Yorkshire).[2]

Mother: They've got Aunties that're quite close, we've got a cousin that lives sort of down the same block ... and er, we've all got the same set of rules in a way ... so we all try to er, be the same with each other's children, ('working class', urban metropolitan area, Yorkshire).

In contrast, some women from local authority housing estates argued that they experience pressures from other mothers to give their children more independence at an earlier age than they believe to be safe. Although some try to resist this local culture by endeavouring to prevent their children playing with those who come from 'families' with a less protectionist attitude towards safety. Kelley et al. (1997) suggest that in part, such differences between middle class and lower income mothers' attitudes to independent outdoor play, may reflect the fact that curtailing children's use of space outside the home is more difficult for women living in cramped homes or houses which are in disrepair and therefore contain physical and social dangers for children which they do not have the money to resolve.

> Mother: I mean I used to think I was a very strange parent because I wouldn't let them out and like kids all say to me 'Why can't we go out, our mates are out?'. I said 'Well, I said their parents don't know where they are'. I mean its, for instance there's a girl that lives round the corner, she is 11 I think she is, and she's had a front door key since she was 8 and her Mum and Dad go to work and leave her with a door key and things like that (Mother, 'working class', urban metropolitan borough, Greater Manchester).

> Mother: I won't say its pressure, I mean sometimes I get a few funny looks [from other mothers] if I say 'No they're not allowed', or something like that. And they say 'Oh well, you've got to have a little bit of time to yourself, you know, you've got to let them go sometime', and you get that sort of attitude round here. Well that's fine, I'm not telling you to keep them in as long as you don't tell me that I've got to let mine wander out – you know, you work your way, I'll do it my way ... I mean if they don't like it well they can lump it can't they, that's the sort of attitude I've got ('working class', urban non-metropolitan borough, Cheshire).

In rural areas there were clear differences in attitudes to children's safety between those mothers who were long-term residents of the countryside and those who were recent incomers. The incomers argued that they all shared the same cautious attitude to their children's safety, adopting similar spatial boundaries. These were contrasted with the more lax parenting practices of long-term residents. The incomers explained these differences by claiming that as a result of their geographical mobility they were more 'worldly wise' and hence more aware of possible dangers than those who have lived in the countryside all their lives. Paradoxically, therefore, the incomers' global knowledge appears to shrink, rather than expand, their children's local worlds. Other processes of sameness and othering were also evident in relation to the micro geography of the village. Those living on the margins of the village claimed to adopt the same limitations on their children as each other, yet these were contrasted with the less restrictive boundaries established by parents living in the centre of the village whose closer proximity to the shops and the Rec. (area of park near the council housing) was claimed to facilitate their ability to 'keep an eye on' their children. Such differences in parenting cultures are described by these mothers:

> Mother: I think the circle we seem to mix with are all fairly sort of careful, um, I suppose we all behave in a similar sort of way ... but I mean I, people do, you know, you see there are certain children in the village who seem to be forever playing on the village green on their own or wandering around, you know, at what would appear to be quite late at night ... and I suppose you don't think too highly of their parents ('middle class', incomer, rural village, Derbyshire).

Mother: I think perhaps people who've lived in the village all their lives are a bit more lenient than us incomers who've come from towns and are perhaps a bit more aware ... And perhaps families who've always played out and always known everybody in the village will let their children play out rather more readily than we do. And also this end of, I mean it's ridiculous isn't it – in a tiny village like this and we sort of talk about 'this end of the village' and the 'middle of the village' but people who are kind of more in the middle and nearer the greens and things, it's easier for them to let them out in the middle of the village than us who are sort of at one end ... I don't feel like an outsider, but I feel, I don't mean this to sound vicious – but I feel a bit more worldly wise. [Much later in the interview she returned to the theme of outsideness saying:] Like people who've been here all their lives, whereas I've lived in different countries and different towns and met up with lots more people, you know, they [long-term residents] can have a very narrow life ('middle class', incomer, rural village, Derbyshire).

In all the neighbourhoods mothers whose childcare beliefs and practices are out of step with local 'norms' are marginalised and excluded. One couple ('biological' mother and 'social father') claimed (in a long and very complicated story) that their daughter had been hurt by a boy who was allowed to roam freely round the village by his parents. When the girl's 'social' father went to complain to the boy's father he was threatened with a wrench. Two years later the parents have still not spoken to each other. Consequently, some women restrict their children's use of space in ways which they do not really believe to be necessary, whilst others give their offspring greater licence than they would ideally like them to have, in order to fit in with local 'common-sense' constructions of what it means to be a 'good mother'. In other words, parenting decisions are often made not on the basis of perceived risks but in order to avoid potential blame.

Lone mothers, in particular, experience difficulties living up to idealised images of motherhood and constructions of 'normality' and 'common-sense' parenting. As Cindi Katz (1993) has pointed out, being able to afford childcare, safe access to outdoor space and a safe living environment is a class privilege. While many lone parents endeavour to bring up their children in accord with two parent household notions of 'safety' and 'good parenting', the reality of managing alone is that mothers (the majority of lone parents are female) often have to give their children more independence than they would ideally like to because they have no partner to share the physical, emotional or financial burden with. These women describe their experiences of managing alone:

Mother: I mean I had one of them [children] that one night decided she was going to go off, my middle one again, and there was no telling where she'd gone and it got to nine o'clock. And I couldn't go out cos I was on my own and I'd got the other three, so I couldn't, two of them were in bed ... anyway a neighbour went looking for her and dragged her back ('working class', urban non-metropolitan borough, Cheshire).

Mother: Sometimes I think I go too strict and at other times I'm not strict enough. But it lapses you know when you've had enough and they're in and out and in and out and you say 'oh go off and play'. That's when you run into problems cos they do run off and play don't they? ('working class', urban metropolitan borough, Greater Manchester).

Mother: You see I'm a single parent and you tend to feel that pressure a little bit more. It doesn't worry me but I do think people judge you in a different way as to whether you are doing a good job or not. I am aware of that ('working class', rural village, Derbyshire).

As the shape of families change through separation, divorce and the introduction of 'social' parents into the household, mothers (who usually remain the prime carers of children) often have to enter into different negotiations about how their children should be cared for. In these circumstances children's safety can be a major source of tension between ex-partners and between women and their new partners. As these quotations demonstrate mothers sometimes find it hard to maintain consistent spatial boundaries for their children and to ensure that their offspring are kept out of danger in public space because their ex-husbands or new partners have different views about the children's safety.

Mother: When I am concerned about her safety is actually when I haven't got any kind of control over it and that's when she's seeing her Dad, my ex-husband because I don't, I don't believe that he has the same um attitude. He's got a different outlook on safety … I know that um, she's seen him and they've spent time say in the pub and she's been allowed to, she's obviously got bored to tears in the pub and what have you, come out, and been allowed to come out and go and watch a local, um, game on a field anyway. Now I would never in a million years let her do anything like that, um, so er, sometimes when it's out of me control I'm bothered about it ('middle class', urban metropolitan borough, Greater Manchester).

Mother: He's [her ex partner, the children's father] totally irresponsible … Totally useless … when I talk about abduction it frightens me, it's wrong to slag him off but he's not, he's not got mothers' instincts … But he takes them to Fun Fairs on Sundays, you know, Camelot, that type of thing and I know he goes on rides with Joe [their son] and Lauren's [their daughter] sat on the bottom waiting, that frightens me. Um – anybody could just walk off with her … he's quite irresponsible … you're on edge all the time thinking will they come home, will he get them back alive? I'm more worried about him [the father] than the stranger ('middle class', urban metropolitan borough, Greater Manchester).

'Social Father': I think you [to the mother] shield them too much.
Mother: I think it's because I've been a single parent you know quite a while, must have been split up from my husband, cos Steve's not moved in that long, we've been together but lived apart. And in the weeks I've been on my own with them

and the responsibility of one person looking after them all them hours, you do tend to over protect them you know. It's so easy for couples to say you know, when they come in, right, you can have them for half an hour but I had them all day for about three years … that's why I'm overprotective with them ('working class', rural village, Derbyshire).

Mother: Well he ['Social Father'] thinks I'm overprotective, which I am I think. I mean I agree with him, I am overprotective but he's, he's only lived in the country all his life and I mean I don't think he realises what dangers are out there you know, whereas I do. I mean he's only their step-dad and I mean he's never had children before … so he just thinks of it like it was when he was little where you were allowed to go anywhere as long as your Mum knew where you were, but no, I know I'm overprotective. I mean it was only him really that Debbie's got as much freedom as she has, you know, because he keeps saying 'Oh you know, other kids 'll torment her', so I give in and she goes out ('working class', rural town, Derbyshire).

The Culture and Conduct of Fatherhood

LaRossa (1988) suggests that it is important to draw a distinction between the culture of fatherhood – the social construction and shared beliefs about men's parenting; and the conduct of fatherhood – what men actually do. He identifies three distinct phases in the culture of fatherhood since the mid nineteenth century. The mid nineteenth to twentieth centuries was a period when the father was the breadwinner, responsible for providing for his family. From the 1940s to 1965, LaRossa (1988) identifies a shift in the culture of fatherhood as fathers came to be perceived as male role models for their children. Since this period, he argues that there has been another shift in the culture of fatherhood with fathers becoming more involved with their offspring, and ascribed a more nurturing role. This latter shift in the culture of fatherhood appears to be partially a response to changes in the conduct of motherhood. It is now more acceptable, and indeed commonplace, for mothers to have paid work outside the home, in turn men are being credited with taking up the domestic slack. The reality however, is that this gap in childcare is more often filled by child minders, au pairs, nannies, play schemes or institutional activities (see Chapter Five), than by fathers (Gregson and Lowe 1993, Smith 1994, Holloway 1994). This leads LaRossa (1988: 451) to suggest that 'the culture of fatherhood has changed more rapidly than the conduct'.

The popular impression of contemporary fathers is that they spend more time with their children than their own fathers or grandfathers did (LaRossa 1988). Fathers now appear to recognise the need to 'do time' with their kids and are proud of the things they do (like changing nappies or taking the children to school). Middle class men, in particular, Thompson and Walker (1989) claim, are both anxious about their 'performance' of fatherhood but also smug because they think that they do more than their own fathers did. However, research suggests that whilst fathers are spending more time with their children in public, creating a perception of 'the new man', this 'work' is largely being done in the company of their partners. Men do not appear to have significantly increased the amount of time they spend alone with their children (La Rossa 1988, Jensen 1994). Phoenix and Woollett (1991: 4) for example, cite six major studies in support of their claim that '[T]he majority of fathers who live with their children do not take responsibility for childcare nor are they involved with their children as much as mothers are'. Where men in dual earner households do relatively more family work than those in single-career families, it is often not because they are choosing to do more, but because their partners do less than full-time homemakers (Thompson and Walker 1989).

The time fathers spend with their offspring, is often time that is not completely focused on the children. Rather, they care for them in the process of being engaged in their own activities, for example, they drop the children off at school on their way to work. In contrast, mothers spend a lot of their time totally devoted to their sons and daughters. As Phoenix and Woollett (1991: 4) point out '[t]o know that a man is a father is generally less informative about how he spends his time and energies than to know that a woman is a mother'. When fathers do focus on their children it is usually to indulge in pleasurable activities, such as watching television or playing football with them. This 'family work' generally takes place at weekends. It tends to be women who alter their schedules during the week to fit in with or look after their children and who deal with children's doctors and schools not men. As such anything that a father does in this way tends to be noticed and assumes a significance disproportionate to his actual involvement (Boulton 1983).

For example, a study of parental involvement with children comparing mothers' and fathers' engagement, accessibility and accountability (responsibility for the child's welfare) found that fathers spend a third of the time that mothers do with their offspring (Lamb 1987). It is mothers, regardless of whether they are in full-time work or not, who bear the brunt (over 90 per cent) of the responsibility for children's welfare – keeping track of where they are, educating them about stranger-dangers and teaching them to cross the road. Whilst fathers are doing some childcare activities, it is mothers who are still doing the lion's share of the nitty-gritty caring work. Although 'absent fathers' are often blamed by some politicians and popular press for producing ill disciplined children (see also Chapter Six), relatively little attention is paid to fathers who frequently work away from home or whose jobs keep them out of the house for most of their children's day (Hardyment 1990). As LaRossa (1988: 455) argues 'the culture and conduct of fatherhood appear to be out of sync'.

This certainly appears to be the case in relation to parenting and children's safety. Whilst 'middle class' fathers were anxious to point out that they played an active role in their children's lives (see the quotation below) they actually appeared to take minimal responsibility for their children's safety. In the majority of households women made it clear where the true division of labour lies, pointing out that they do most of the emotional and practical work of teaching children about risks and managing their safety.[3]

> Mother: Things have changed haven't they. Clive's always been involved with everything, he used to have to do the nappy bucket when we had Lucy and didn't have disposable nappies.
> Father: Our youngest daughter's been off today hasn't she, off school today and if ever they're ill I'm always the one that has to look after them. I am the one that would normally nurse them ('middle class', urban non-metropolitan borough, Cheshire).

> Mother: Colin doesn't, he's not quite as involved with the children as I am. He's busy outside quite a lot and like he never knows, he should do really, but he never knows whether it's ballet or beavers or cubs or what night, where they're going. He doesn't know where they really are. It's me that takes control whereas, well I don't know what the cows are doing [he is a farmer], you see [laughs] that's his side and I kind of sort the children out [although she is in paid employment as well] ('middle class', rural village, Derbyshire).

Whilst mothers, under daily pressure from children to relax their boundaries are often flexible about (re)negotiating their children's spatial ranges, fathers (from all backgrounds) tend to hold a more consistent line – to be stricter. This can lead to tension when they discover that the children have been given more freedom to go out than they would like them to have as these quotations illustrate.

> Father: I don't like Sally going out by herself.
> Mother: He doesn't like Sally going out full-stop.
> Interviewer: Is that because she is the youngest or because she is a girl?
> Father: No, I was exactly the same with Paul when he first started. I didn't like it when Phillip first started to go by himself.
> Mother: But they went by themselves at a much earlier age.
> Father: Well I didn't like it even then. I told her [to interviewer] I never liked it then. That wasn't with my approval they went. It was just something you [to wife] did ('middle class', rural village, Derbyshire).

> Mother: He's far worse than me, him. At least I have some, what's the word, I let her have some freedom, yeah. He doesn't, he thinks she's about two dunn'he [to older children], sometimes he does honestly, he's terrible with her … it's very much a case of 'Don't think we need bother telling your Dad you went up town or you went to flaming such a place with Clare [laughing]'. And she's not daft. She doesn't tell him cos she knows if she tells him she'll get her flaming ear bent for half an hour … , so no, he's far worse than me ('working class', urban metropolitan borough, Greater Manchester).

Mother: I'm at work sometimes at night, you're [to her partner] in charge aren't you?
'Social Father': She's very soft with them sometimes though, let's them get away with murder don't you?
Mother: You [to him] have to be quiet don't you, have to keep your mouth shut sometimes don't you duck?
'Social Father': Have to bite my lip.
Mother: I am soft, I don't know what ... my Dad was same, my Mum was soft and Dad were very strict ('working class', rural village, Derbyshire).

Mother: I let them off and their Dad says they can't and I say they can ... He's so, he thinks children have to grow up like he grew up and they don't [laughs] ... He tries to be more disciplined but I end up saying you know you've got to think about this and this and this and I get away with getting them off a lot more ('middle class', urban metropolitan borough, Greater Manchester).

When mothers cannot be persuaded to be lenient, children often resist and actively transgress the boundaries imposed on them by their parents (a point returned to in Chapter Four). In response parents appear to adopt different disciplinary styles. Mothers commonly rely on verbal reasoning, whilst fathers claim to take on a more 'traditional' authoritarian role. This ties in with sociological research which suggests that men use physical punishment, shouting or threats, more often than women (Hart and Robinson 1994) and that mothers tend to be more opposed to physical punishment than fathers (Holden and Zambarano 1992). Low income families are also more likely to use physical discipline than 'middle class' families (Peterson et al. 1994). Fathers, however, tend to hit daughters less often than sons and to strike all children less after the age of 11 (Newson and Newson 1976) which is undoubtedly related to the fact that children become larger and are more able to resist their punishment, or hit back at this age (Hood William 1990).

The traditional 'wait till your father gets home' warning is, it appears, still a potent threat. The majority of the fathers (from all backgrounds) interviewed argued that because they spend less time during the day with their children than their partners, that they are more distanced from domestic disputes between mothers and children. This means that they are more easily able to discipline their offspring when they transgress the spatial boundaries imposed on them, and unlike mothers, fathers claim to strictly enforce the punishments dealt out to their children. It is a representation of the gender division of parenting that was supported by the majority of women.

Mother: They do get smacked when they push us to the limit ... they are more scared of their Dad, they're a lot more frightened of him and they'll listen to him a lot easier than what they, I can break my back saying the same thing again, and again and again and then when I go mad, then they'll listen. But they're more, they are more fearful of their Dad ('working class', urban metropolitan area, Yorkshire).

Father: I'm the strictest but she'll [his wife], she like to say something but he knows that he can get away with his mother which he can't get away with me you see, like on Mondays I don't finish until about three ... and Salem can do anything with his mother but when it comes about three o'clock he apologises to his mother saying 'oh Dad's coming now I will apologise I'm very sorry', yeah. They're crafty you know kids, very crafty nowadays, you know what I mean ('working class', urban metropolitan area, Yorkshire).

Father: And the girls know that if they do wrong they'll get smacked for it, even Sarah at 12 years of age you know. They know that they've got that little bit of leeway with Kath [his wife] and Kath says to me sometimes that they've been doing this, that and the other, I said 'why don't you do something about it?' and it's always left to me. I always remember when me Dad – I could twirl me Mum a bit but whenever me Dad came into the house that was it then. It was a little bit of fear as well but it always brought me up in good stead you know, I've always believed in what he did was right, although sometimes I was a bit scared. And the girls have admitted to me sometimes that they've been a bit scared of me. I've never bruised them or anything like that but I'll always give them a good slap if they've done wrong ('middle class', non metropolitan area, Cheshire).

Father: I'm not here very much so I have the advantage of being able to walk in, sort of look cleanly at a situation without having any emotional involvement in the situation, sorting it all out – I tend to be probably stricter on them. I also have a lot shorter temper so they know if they push it with me they're really asking for it (rural village, 'middle class', Derbyshire).

The exceptions to this gender division of parenting were mainly evident in households where the mother was a full-time homemaker. As women quoted below explain they primarily discipline the children because the children are their responsibility, although different personality characteristics in some households accounted for why some mothers were stricter than fathers.

Mother: I think the majority of the time I'm the disciplinarian in this house, but the odd time when he raises his voice, they do take as much notice of him as they do of me. But because I'm here more I think I do more of the discipline than he does ('middle class', urban non-metropolitan area).

Mother: I think, the way our life works, Rick works and I do, it's a sort of very stereotyped sexist role, he works, I do the home, but this is the way our life works ... I tend to be in charge of the children ... I'm a fairly assertive and aggressive person, I think probably [laughs]. Rick is very passive, whereas he is very self confident he's not as, I shout a lot, Rick doesn't shout at all ... I think I get by on volume sometimes ('middle class', rural area, Derbyshire).

Tensions between some mothers and 'social fathers' were also evident in relation to disciplining responsibilities. On the one hand several mothers argued that because the children are 'theirs', that they alone should discipline them. This was also tied up with a concern that the children were maybe more resentful of being punished by their 'social parent'. On the other hand, other mothers, as earlier quotations indicated, argued that following the break-up of their marriages they had been too 'soft' on their children and therefore they hand over much of the responsibility for punishing their children to the children's 'social fathers'.

In summary, this chapter has shown that safety is an important part of popular discourses about how parents should raise their children. Parents negotiate and establish the extent of their children's personal geographies according to their understandings of what restrictions a 'good parent' should impose on their youngsters and according to their perceptions of their offspring's competence to avoid or cope with 'public' dangers. This process of negotiating children's spatial boundaries and disciplining them for any infringements is highly gendered.

Traditionally, girls have been perceived as more at risk in public space than boys. Significantly, however, this research suggests that parents hold a more complex and contradictory view of gender and siblings than previous studies have suggested. In particular, girls appear to be perceived as more capable of negotiating public space safely than boys because they are perceived to have greater self awareness, sexual maturity and a sense of responsibility than their brothers. In a reversal of 'traditional' constructions of masculinity, boys are perceived as innocent, irrational, irresponsible and as increasingly vulnerable to violence from peers and adolescents. These complex constructions of gender were evident amongst parents from different class and ethnic back-grounds, contradicting racialised discourses which frequently represent Asian young women as passive and vulnerable in public space. Although this is not to deny the significance of patriarchy in south Asian young women's lives (see, for example, Brah 1993).

Whilst parental attitudes to gender and safety appear to be changing, this research suggests that parenting is still conducted largely on traditional gender lines, with mothers bearing the burden of caring and supervising their children on a daily basis, whilst the father, in most households, still carries out the disciplinary role. This despite the fact that the culture of fatherhood and the conduct of motherhood have both shifted significantly in recent decades. The importance of place, class and ethnic identities were also evident in the construction of 'local norms' about what it means to be a 'good' mother.

The gender division of childcare responsibilities appear to be more complicated in reconstituted families where parenting is shared between 'biological' mothers and fathers who live apart, and 'social' fathers. Tensions were particularly evident in relation to whether 'biological' fathers can be trusted to take adequate safety precautions when the children are in their care and in relation to the role of 'social' fathers in the care and disciplining of their partners' children.

The following chapter develops these themes further by looking at how children's competence is performed and contested through everyday interactions between household members; and how children resist parental restrictions on their use of space.

Notes

1 These represent just two of many ways that the conduct of motherhood has changed. For example, other influences include women's changing access to private transport and childcare.
2 In four out of the ten interviews with parents of Asian origin the father spoke for both parents or the father or a child interpreted the mother's response.
3 This was also implicit in the different contributions mothers and fathers made in the interviews. Whilst fathers often spoke for longer and sometimes completely dominated proceedings they were often making general statements or comments, it was the women were the ones that largely talked about the nitty-gritty of their children's everyday lives. This sometimes led to tensions between mothers' and fathers' accounts. For a discussion of these issues see Valentine 1999a.

Chapter 4

'I can handle it':
Children and Competence

Chapters Two and Three have focused on parents' risk assessments in relation
to children's safety, and the role of gender and parenting cultures in shaping
these risk agendas. However, children commonly have different perceptions
of their own safety from their parents; and want, as well as facing peer group
pressures, to stay out further and longer than their parents usually allow.
Children's spatial ranges are therefore a product of constant household
negotiations with their parents about their 'competence' to negotiate public
space safely. This chapter explores these negotiations. It begins by outlining
the concepts of competence and performance. It then considers these in
relation to the processes through which parents establish children's spatial
ranges, and associated boundaries. The chapter then switches from a focus
on parents' views, to consider children's own social worlds, by looking at
how children attempt to 'perform' and negotiate their competence and their
tactics to subvert or resist the spatial restrictions imposed on them. The
discussion involves consideration of the way that children exploit power
dynamics between adults in different household forms, and their attitudes to
their parents' social competence. In doing so it demonstrates the instability
and contested meanings of the binary concepts – 'adult' and 'child'. The
final section of the chapter considers the way that similar issues of risk,
competence, boundary setting and subversion, are also played out in relation
to children's on-line activities in cyberspace.

Competence and Performance

The chapter emphasises two theoretical concepts: 'competence' and
'performance'.
    The dominant understanding of childhood in contemporary western society
remains one of a linear sequence of developmental stages in which children's
behaviour progressively evolves from simplicity to complexity, from
irrationality to rationality (despite the fact that adulthood is a social construct
not merely a matter of physical maturity) on the path to adulthood (Prout and
James 1990). This is an understanding of childhood that owes much to the
work of Piaget (1952, 1971). Rather than viewing intelligence as innate he
believed that it develops through complex interactions between a child and

its environment (Aitken 1994). Using a range of empirical experiments, he developed a model of four stages of intellectual growth.

More recently, this work has been criticised, particularly by feminists and poststructuralists, on empirical and theoretical grounds. First, it has been argued that Piaget's experiments merely measured children's ability to make sense of the tasks he set them, rather than their actual intellectual abilities. Donaldson (1978) for example, has shown that if Piaget's tests are presented to children in more child-friendly ways then children demonstrate higher levels of competence than those recorded by Piaget's methods. Likewise, ethnographic studies in schools show children's abilities extend beyond their developmental capabilities (Epstein 1993). Second, Piaget has been criticised for ignoring the socio-cultural context of children's lives, which it is argued can foster or hinder, the stages of a child's development. For example, Gergen et al. (1990) have demonstrated the way that cultural beliefs about appropriate ways to bring up children affect parents' child rearing practices and hence child development patterns. In their study they found that German and American mothers strongly subscribed to the linear model of child development. This Gergen et al. (1990) argued was not a product of the mothers' observation of the 'true nature of the child' but rather was a result of their own cultural beliefs.

However, despite being subject to these and other critiques (see, for example, Walkerdine 1984), Piaget's linear sequence of development model remains significant in shaping popular understandings of children's competence. In other words, children are understood to be merely in the process of becoming, they are not considered 'complete' (Blitzer 1991). It is not that they are regarded as different from adults but rather as less than adults. As Waksler (1986: 74) argues '[I]n everyday life we adults take for granted that children *as a category* know *less* than adults, have *less* experience, are *less* serious, and are *less* important than adults'. It is a point echoed by Alanen (1990: 16) who claims that '[t]he child, for social theory, remains *negatively defined*: defined not by what the child *is*, but by what he or she is *not* but is subsequently going to be. The child is depicted as pre-social, potentially social, in the process of becoming social.'

One consequence of this conceptualisation of children's competence is that in both everyday life, and academic research, there is a tendency to ignore children's own experiences and understandings of the world (Waksler 1986). For example, within the law children are commonly held to be unreliable witnesses, whilst within academia they are often perceived as incapable of making rational judgements or voicing a sensible opinion. Qvortrup (1994: 4) observes 'the adult world does not recognize children's praxis, because competence is defined merely in relation to adults' praxis'. In this way, 'modern childhood constructs children out of society, mutes their voices, denies their personhood, limits their potential' (Ennew 1994). While these understandings of childhood – in terms of both physical and social immaturity – obviously have some purchase and common sense value, they do not provide an adequate explanation of children's lifeworlds or how they become adults (Mayall 1994). As such, new social studies of childhood (e.g. Prout and James 1990) focus on exploring children's own explanations of their lives. The emphasis within this work is on recognising the level of sophistication that young people demonstrate in managing their own social relations and on considering the ways that children resist the childhood, which is imposed on them by adults (e.g. Waksler 1986, Qvortrup 1994). At the heart of this approach is a recognition of children's competence, that children are responsible social actors in their own right, adept at managing their own space and time, that they are 'agents of their own life' (Alanen 1990: 20). Obvious examples of this include the way that youngsters may act as interpreters for their parents, use technology such as videos and computers which baffle less adept adults (Holloway and Valentine 2001a), and make choices about their own medical treatment (Alderson and Goodwin 1993).

The second concept that is important in this chapter is that of performance (see also Chapters One and Six). The concept of performance is derived from the work of the feminist philosopher Judith Butler. In *Gender Trouble: Feminism and the Subversion of Identity*, Butler (1990) rejects the idea that biology is a bedrock that underlies the categories of gender and sex. Rather she theorises gender (and implicitly other identities too) as performative. She argues that 'gender is the repeated stylization of the body, a set of repeated acts within a highly rigid regulatory framework that congeal over time to produce the appearance of substance, of a natural order of being' (Butler 1990: 33). In other words, Butler (1990) theorises gender as an unstable and permanently contested category. In this chapter, age is also considered, like gender, to be a performative act that is naturalized through repetition and therefore is both fluid and contested.

The following two sections of the chapter explore the mutual and intertwined ways that grown-ups and children negotiate and define their respective competencies as parents and social actors; and the role that notions of 'performance' and contestation play in this.

Parents' Understandings of Children's Competence

Chapter Two highlighted parents' fears for children's safety in public space. At the heart of these concerns is a belief that children are not competent to negotiate space alone because they are unable to understand what danger they might encounter at the hands of strangers and will not take appropriate avoidance action when confronted by potential abductors. In particular, parents claim that children are unable to grasp concepts of inappropriate touch and sexual violence (although this may, in part at least, be related to the way children are educated about personal safety: see Chapter Two). Unable or unwilling to trust their children to manage their own safety in public places, most parents actively control and restrict their children's use of space. For example, a US survey found that of 323 seven to ten year olds questioned, only 16 per cent were allowed to go further than their own block unaccompanied by an adult. These negotiations about spatial ranges are effectively negotiations about competence and take place at many different levels – both through explicit discussion between parents and their offspring and between parents and their friends and relatives (see also the discussion of parenting cultures, Chapter Three) but also more abstractly through reference to conceptions (which change over space and time) of what it is appropriate for children to be able to do at different ages. This father explains:

> Father: Richard's eight and he's not responsible enough to go to the shops on his own, so no he can't. If in six months' time he suddenly becomes responsible at home, then OK, fair enough. So it's not exact, an age, it's the actual child themselves ('middle class', urban non-metropolitan borough).

As this quote hints, by performing or demonstrating competence in one aspect of their lives children can use evidence of this 'maturity' to try to negotiate more independence in other contexts (Valentine 1997b). In particular, children use performative strategies in the private sphere of the home, such as cleaning their bedroom or helping in the kitchen, as levers to win more autonomy from their parents in public space. While sometimes this strategy may be successful, on other occasions parents do not let the definition of a child's competence in one space, spill over into another. Rather, understandings of children's maturity in public and private can stand in awkward contradiction to each other. For example, this mother explains how she trusts her son sufficiently to allow him to take on responsibilities in the kitchen in an environment full of domestic hazards but does not let him walk to school alone.

> Mother: He knows it's about trust and about being honest, about – he'll only get those freedoms as he shows me he's capable of accepting those responsibilities. You start them within the home, giving him responsibilities, and building them up. I mean he makes toast and the next thing I want him to start learning is how to use the rings, the hobs, you know. Then when I know he can accept responsibility I'll actually start allowing him to go to school and back on his own (lone parent, 'working class', urban non-metropolitan area).

In the majority of cases – although there were a few exceptions – parents employed tougher and stricter measures of their children's competence in public space before they allowed their offspring a semblance of independence, than they adopted in private space. This illustrates the extent to which contemporary parents consider stranger-dangers to be more important than domestic threats to their children's safety (see also Chapter Two). Indeed, parents sometimes used 'stranger-danger' warnings to restrict their children's use of space, despite the fact that their children were deemed more 'grown up' in other situations. This was not because they were necessarily anxious about their children's 'streetwise' skills but rather because of anxieties that their offspring would get in with the wrong social crowd or become involved in drugs (a point returned to in Chapter Six).

Some parents also argued that children do not have the social skills or 'savvy' to distinguish between 'good' and 'bad' people and consequently are too naive and not responsible or mature enough to recognise potentially dangerous situations and to deal with them appropriately, as this mother explains:

> Mother: I mean I sort of said to him about you know, um, some people you know, will try and hurt children, you know but it's very difficult to say what could happen um you know without telling them too much ... It's a bit difficult to expect them to understand it all ('working class', rural area).

As well as an assumption that competence increases with age, parents also argued that levels of children's competence are highly gendered. Although previous research has suggested that girls use of space is more restricted than boys (Hart 1979, Bjorklid 1985), as Chapter Three demonstrated, the evidence of this research is that a growing number of parents are equally concerned for their sons' and daughters' safety but whereas daughters (and girls in general) are commonly described as sensible, logical and therefore responsible enough to manage their own safety, boys are commonly represented as easily led, irrational, slow to mature and consequently as less capable of negotiating public space alone than. Indeed, parents justified their claims about differences in their children's competence to deal with strangers by recounting anecdotes which illustrated gender differences in their offsprings' performance of responsibility in other contexts, for example, in relation to racial abuse, domestic safety, saving money and so on. Following a complex story about her daughter dealing with racism one mother said:

> Mother: I was just proud of the way she handled it and for me. Yeah for me Nazreen [daughter], anything, anything that happens that's actually racist ... she'll stand up for what she believes in. Whereas Retan [son], if somebody actually said that to him he would have hit 'em. He'd have just, that's the way, that's his way of dealing with it. Nazreen, no, she'll like talk her way through it, she's more logical thinking, more sensible, Retan'll like hit and talk afterwards ('working class', urban metropolitan area).

While some parents actively try to develop their children's autonomy and streetwise skills, for example, by giving them special 'licences' to make specific journeys, others are more cautious, keeping their offspring under covert surveillance. These experimental tests of competence are important means through which children can renegotiate their spatial boundaries and can (re)define their 'age'. These parents explain:

Father: If they do go for a while anyway we will get hold of the dog chain, get hold of the dog and go for a walk down there just to see what they are doing. We are quite fortunate cause Mum and Dad live on the other side of the bank. So they can look down. We can see Mum and Dad's house from where we live.

Mother: Mum gets the binoculars out. If we ring up and say is Simon still down on the tip? She would say 'hang on a minute I'll go and get me glasses out' ('middle class', urban metropolitan borough).

Mother: [when her daughter started walking to school with friends] I used to hide around the corner like a Japanese sniper [sic] and I used to go, I used to watch them … and then run. I used to have to run like the clappers before she came strolling down otherwise you see that would cause a row. But just for a couple of weeks I watched her do that ('middle class', urban metropolitan borough).

The boundaries parents establish with their youngsters in this way appear to depend not only on their perceptions of competence in relation to the age and gender of the child but were also shaped by parental perceptions of their own locality in terms of the social make-up of their neighbourhood (in relation to 'class' and 'race' tensions, drugs, crime, vandalism, gang violence and so on) and the physical characteristics of the environment (such as proximity to parks, alleys or places where their children may get into 'social' trouble as well as physical dangers).

These evaluations in turn are influenced by the time of day and year. Night-time is considered more dangerous because the people who dominate public space change and therefore so too does the nature of space (Valentine 1989) and time of year. Children also have more freedom in the summer when daylight hours are longer; and in the vacation when their parents may be at work most of the day. Finally as Chapter Two highlighted, knowledge of local incidents and parents own social and cultural values also feed into this equation (Perez and Hart 1980, Parkinson 1987). For example, in one urban non-metropolitan area a well publicised spate of attempted (but unsuccessful) child abductions in the local area caused some of the parents interviewed to redefine their children's spatial ranges. Prior to these incidents some had considered their children capable of walking to and from school alone or with friends. These understandings of the children's competence were subsequently (re)negotiated in the light of the publicity about the failed abduction attempts. As Chapter Three illustrated, it is through these routine practices of parenting that understandings of children's competence and therefore what it means to be a 'good' or competent parent are performed and contested over both space and time (Dyck 1989, 1990), producing distinct local parenting cultures and common-sense understandings of local geographies of risk.

Even where parents are confident in their children's competence to manage their own safety they sometimes continue to impose restrictions on their spatial ranges because they are acutely conscious that mothers and fathers are held responsible for their offspring's well-being long after they have actually demonstrated that they are competent to negotiate public space alone. In particular, examples were cited where the media had blamed those whose children were abducted for being incompetent parents (see Chapter Two). It is a point which has also been taken up by Kitzinger (1990) who cites a number of examples of the media holding bereaved parents accountable for their loss, including press coverage of multiple child murders in Atlanta, Georgia, in which the headline 'where were these children's mothers?' appeared. In a similar case in the UK the press lambasted the mother of a girl kidnapped en route to a bus stop for not chaperoning her daughter (Elliott 1988: 25). Not surprisingly some parents reproduced similar opinions. This mother comments:

> Mother: When you hear about children abducted or things happening a lot of the time I think it is the parents' fault not knowing where the child is or letting the child go too far ('middle class', rural commuter 'village').

It is clear then from this discussion that repetitive acts of parenting which involve setting boundaries, supervision/care and discipline and which take place within a regulatory framework (e.g. the gaze of others, local parenting cultures; the media etc.) all congeal to produce the appearance of 'proper' or 'normal' local levels of children's competence and 'proper' or 'normal' local levels of parental competence.[1] This is not to imply however, that parents are necessarily consistent either over space and time, between children, or in their understanding of children's competence in relation to their safety outside the home versus their safety inside the home.

Most mothers and fathers initially presented an ideal account in the interviews of their arrangements for setting boundaries, supervising and disciplining their children. But often these accounts proceeded to unravel in discussions as it became apparent that being a parent is an experience riddled with inconsistencies and contradictions (for example, between the way that one child is dealt with across space and time, and the way that siblings are treated). As Chapter Three touched on, mothers, in particular, confessed to giving into children's attempts to push back their spatial boundaries because they are distracted by domestic pressures, or as a last resort to shut the kids up. Similarly, several lone parents, overstretched because they do not have anyone to share the constant burden of parenting with, also recognise the disparities, which sometimes occur between their ideal level of supervision and the realities of where their children are allowed to go unaccompanied by an adult. Sharing children with an estranged partner also means that many lone parents cannot be as consistent in maintaining their children's spatial ranges as they would like because of the different practices, boundaries or disciplining strategies adopted by the other parent.

Importantly, children's spatial ranges also appear to expand but then sometimes to contract again, either because the child failed to live up to the level of responsibility they had been credited with or because parent(s) found it necessary to pacify younger siblings by restoring parity between their offsprings' boundaries. As Solberg (1990: 120) points out '[c]onceptually therefore, children may "grow" or "shrink" in age as negotiations take place.' Thus, although, young people are in a weak position when it comes to bargaining with parent(s) about their spatial ranges (and adults have the power to discipline children), children do play an active role in (re)negotiating their parent(s)' understandings of their ability to manage their own lives and play an important part in constructing the competence levels of their own parent(s). It is these processes that are considered in the next section of this chapter.

Children's Performance of Competence

As previous work has demonstrated, children want to and are, very competent and adept at managing their own lifeworlds (Alanen 1988, Thorne 1987). This is evident in relation to the issue of personal safety. All the young people who took part in group discussions had had stranger-danger warnings drummed into them at an early age and were extremely competent at repeating them as these girls demonstrate:

> Girl 2: Don't go off with nobody who you don't know. Don't talk to strangers.
> Girl 4: Yeah don't talk to strangers, don't take money or any sweets and don't talk to nobody you don't know.
> Girl 3: And if somebody asks ya do you know where a place is and they say come in my car and show me, don't.
> Girl 2: And don't go to people's houses you don't know (three girls, 'working class', urban non-metropolitan area).

Whilst these were the rules the children had been taught, their understandings of their own safety and their actual fears were more complex. Previous research suggests that young people are fearful for their personal safety. A North American survey (Zill 1983) found that 28 per cent of respondents aged 7–11 were afraid to go out because of a fear of being hurt by another person; 50 per cent said that they had been harassed by adults or children whilst out and 12 per cent had been physically attacked by other young people. A similar study by the UK Home Office in 1992 found that six out of ten 12–15 year olds could recall a recent occasion where they had experienced some kind of assault/harassment – and that one in four of these incidents was assessed as genuinely criminal (Barnados 1994). The evidence of this research however, is that (perhaps not surprisingly) boys were reluctant to acknowledge any fears for their personal safety, reciting stranger-danger warnings in a mocking way as if they were an insult to their physical capabilities. This reinforces the findings of other surveys, which have found that females and younger children (7–10) report more fears than boys and older children (11–13, 14–16 year olds) (e.g. Gullone and King 1993).

Rather than admit to fears, most boys bragged about the dangers in their own neighbourhoods and about petty crimes that they had committed. In particular, children from a local authority housing neighbourhood in a metropolitan area stressed their knowledge, or in some cases alleged experiences of, local drugs and gang violence. For the boys there is prestige and status in having experienced danger (Quadrel et al. 1993). Their greatest concern appears to be 'being bashed' by older teenagers and youths (see also Chapter Six), although most argued they were capable of defending themselves and taunted each other as 'chickens'. In several of the metropolitan housing estates, these fears of other local teenagers/youths were strongly racialized. In common with studies of other neighbourhoods (Webster 1995a, Webster 1995b, Keith 1995, Westwood 1990, Watt and Stenson 1998), the boys identified distinct white and distinct South Asian 'territories' which, they claimed, are aggressively defended against 'outsiders'.

The boys also articulated stereotypical views on the safety of girls, arguing that sisters and female peers were more vulnerable to being 'kidnapped' (their term). One predominantly British South Asian group acknowledged the cultural pressures which also limited their sisters' freedoms to go out alone; whilst another also demonstrated a greater understanding of the sexual element of stranger-danger than parents and schools are often willing to acknowledge (see Chapter Two), arguing that girls are vulnerable to rape.

Like the boys, the girls also argued that they are competent at negotiating their own safety in public space, albeit in a more modest way. In particular, a common argument advanced was that they were safe because they always went everywhere with their friends. Girls from rural areas and from one of the metropolitan local authority housing estates claimed a particular familiarity with their neighbourhood, arguing that they felt safe because there were always houses they could run to if they felt under threat. In contrast, middle-class urban and suburban girls appeared to have less local place knowledge because they spend more of their leisure time indoors or taking part in activities supervised by adults (see Chapter Five). This activity pattern ties in with Newson and Newson's (1976) claim that working class and lower middle class children are expected to spend most of their time outside the home, coming in to relax; whereas middle class children are expected to go outside for exercise and relaxation but then are expected to spend time indoors on school work or more creative activities (a point returned to in Chapter Five).

Unlike the boys, the girls did admit a fear of strangers as this quote illustrates:

> Girl: Like people getting picked up, like by strangers and stuff … Like cars pull up and start asking you questions, so then like you can easy get pulled into a car or anything like that and there's plenty of weird people walking around, hiding in

bushes and parks, so anything really could happen while you were out ('middle class', urban non-metropolitan area).

Despite these anxieties, and being aware of the stranger-danger message, the common impression from all the group discussions was that children of both sexes have a strong sense of invulnerability. The evidence of the psychology literature is that this is a product of a sense of control. In this young people are no different from adults (Perloff 1983). In the cases of the boys they perceive a sense of individual self efficacy, whilst the girls gain self confidence from their friends and from knowing the people and places where they hang out. These networks are also an important source of information. Children are usually treated as if they have less knowledge and less experience than adults, yet young people often have well developed local knowledge of both incidents and rumours of danger and good understanding of local 'place ballets' (Seamon 1979) because of the amount of time they spend in the neighbourhood with local friends. In contrast, many parents who spend all day working away from home and have few local social contacts are often quite incompetent or out of touch with what is going on in their own area as this mother explains:

> Mother: She's probably more likely than me to recognise a stranger, she is um more part of the local community and knows who people are having spent all these years based here, all her life is centred on here so she's more familiar with the local environment and the people who make it up ('middle class', rural town, Derbyshire).

In this way children are often experts in their own lives, making more use of their own detailed local knowledge when negotiating public space than their parents' blanket bans or warnings. In fact, many regard their personal safety as their own (often allied with friends), not their parents' responsibility. As such children do not always comply with their parents' temporal-spatial rules.

A number of studies have demonstrated how children resist the social practices of adults (Willis 1981, Katz 1991). In *Learning to Labour*, a classic ethnographic study of British working-class 'lads' from an industrial area, Paul Willis (1981) explores 'kids' opposition to and subversion of the school system. In cataloguing their counter-school culture ('dossing', 'blagging', 'wagging', 'having a laff' and so on), Willis argues that 'the lads' limit their own opportunities for social mobility, and so reproduce their class position. Likewise, geographical studies (Katz 1991, Breitbart 1998) have also drawn attention to young people's ability to subvert and resist the production of public space in late capitalism. This work has particularly highlighted young people's sense of disconnection from the city, lack of access to public space and their attempts to resist adult oriented urban space through neighbourhood environmental activism and public art.

Young people are not only agents in their own lives at school or on the street, they (including young children) are also active agents in the home, negotiating how parents construct their competence levels and demonstrating an ability to negotiate control in the household and to take part in or influence decision making (Valentine 1999b). As Solberg (1994: 119) has argued, children 'do not passively adapt themselves to what their parents say and do.' Rather they often resist, oppose and find gaps in adult restrictions. One of the most common strategies used by the children to win extensions to their spatial ranges is to demonstrate their competence to parents before asking for permission to change their boundaries. To give one example, a girl wanted to go to the park after tea with her friends but she knew her mother would not give her permission to do this so she did not ask for it. Rather, she deceived her mother to go there. After she had been doing this for sometime she then deliberately 'slipped up' so that her mother would find out. She was then able to argue that the fact that she had been going to and from the park safely for sometime meant that she was now capable of being 'allowed' to go there. Her performative strategy paid off and her mother agreed to accept that she was now competent enough to go to the park with friends.

Children in two parent families also demonstrated a sophisticated knowledge of their parents' relationships, power dynamics and conflict in the household, playing mothers and fathers off against each other. In particular, mothers were often presented as the weak link. As Chapter Three illustrated, mothers spend more time with children and are therefore less consistent in their parenting strategies, are under more domestic and emotional stress than fathers, and consequently are more likely to succumb to sustained pressure from their offspring to extend their spatial ranges. The opportunity to manipulate mothers' and fathers' different attitudes to parenting and parenting roles was especially evident amongst children living in reconstituted families with a 'biological parent' (usually their mother) and a 'social parent'. This strategy appears to be most effectively used by those children who still maintain some contact with their other 'biological parent', as these sorts of multiple kinship relations give children more scope to play the adults in their lives off against each other.

Children also appear to try and play their own parents off against other people's parents, implicitly playing on their anxieties about local parenting 'norms' (see Chapter Three). The more sophisticated amongst the participants were adept at collectively organising to manipulate their parents in this way as these girls explain:

Girl: You say you're at my house, don't you, when you want to come in late. Like you'll phone home and say you're at my house ... yeah that's what I do when I want to come home late, I'll say 'Oh I'm phoning from Gemma's house and staying down there for a bit' and that's what gets me out of going home early ... If there's something you're definitely doing, they think you're doing then they're not worried ('working class', urban metropolitan area, Yorkshire).

Girl: I want her to knock on for me and then if she's no around I ask Rianna to knock on for me and then when me Mum and Dad says 'yeah' [because Rianna's parents have allowed her out] and then I'm allowed out, then I go and knock on for her and then she'll be allowed out [because the speaker's parents have let her out] and then we just go ('working class', British South Asian, urban metropolitan area).

Failing this, children often just break the rules as this girl and boy explain:

Girl: I just keep on asking me Mum 'cos I know me Dad'll say no sometimes and when my Mum, when I ask my Mum and sometimes she says yes, sometimes she says no, so then I wait until she's gone to sleep and then I go out ('working class', urban metropolitan area, Yorkshire).

Boy: I ask me Mum and if she says 'no', then I ask my Dad, if he says 'no' I'll go up to me bedroom window, climb out of the window onto the extension roof, onto the wall and then I go ('working class', urban metropolitan area, Yorkshire).

Just as parents presented their children as naive, gullible and consequently incompetent, many children used the same language of incompetence to describe their parents. They criticised their parents for being irrational, inconsistent and unfair but most importantly as being too naive and trusting and therefore as easy to manipulate.

Although nearly all the parents interviewed claimed that their children had never had a frightening experience, the evident of the focus group discussions carried out with children suggests that young people do have such experiences.

Girl 1: ... Me and Clare were walking around, you know, like it were during holiday in summer and there were always these two cars, like everywhere we went them cars were always like following us ...
Interviewer: So what did you do about that? How did you deal with it?
Girl 2: Well we told Angela and she says next time try and get the number plate ... but you couldn't really, you know ...
Girl 1: No they just drove past us quite a lot and always be in places where we were gonna go, so they must have been following us, like to get there before us and then like whenever we got, they was there, so like we was on us way up here and they was like parked at bottom.
Interviewer: Yeah, did you get scared or how did you, how did you feel? You told Angela but did you tell your mums and your parents?
Girl 1: Well I didn't tell my Mum cos I knew what she'd be like – she wouldn't let me out. She'd have come to pick me up and that and I don't want her to do that ... She worries a right lot my Mum. Slightest little thing she starts worrying [laughter] ... so I just tell her what I have to, there's no point worrying her any more, so I don't tell her ('working class', urban metropolitan area, Yorkshire).

In each case the children handled potentially dangerous situations relatively competently. This bears out to some extent research by Klayman (1985). He compared children's and adults' risk evaluation and decision making skills in similar circumstances and found that children as young as 12 deal with risks in a similar way to adults (Quadrel et al. 1993). In many ways then children are less differentiated from adults than we usually recognise.

Except in extreme cases most children appear to turn to their peers rather than adults for help. One father recognised that this is often due to peer group pressures to be seen to be able to cope without adults. He says:

> Father: You know I think children like to try and sort things out. Round here it's sort of a tough area in'it and if you start getting your parents involved they think well he's a Mummy's or Daddy's boy ('working class', urban metropolitan area, Yorkshire).

A view supported by the comment of these girls:

> Girl 1: Cos like we share everything, all us problems and everything come between us three …
> Girl 2: Yeah like we ask each other advice on what to do all different things and everything … We'll just pass knowledge around but … if its gets serious, I'd go to me Mum or me older sister and get it sorted out ('working class', urban metropolitan area, Yorkshire).

In a further ironic reversal of parents' anxieties about their children's ability to cope; many children conceal 'dangerous' experiences from their parents in order to maintain their parents' innocence and protect them from worry or anxiety. Although this is often underlain by the more pragmatic reason that informing parents of such incidents may lead to the imposition of tighter restrictions on the child. As this girl explains:

> Girl: Mum worries about people and she just, she keeps on worrying about me but I think I'm alright. I think I'm safe but I know, well Mum thinks that I'm not, she picks me up because of people on the streets and that, so I mean I couldn't tell her when me and Emma saw that man [flasher] because she'd have freaked and I'd never have been let out again ('middle class', urban non-metropolitan area, Yorkshire).

In this way children are often actually more competent than they are presumed to be by their parents. The so-called hallmarks of adulthood – maturity, rationality and so on are just as readily performed by a child as a grown-up; whilst as the previous quote demonstrates sometimes adults demonstrate irrational, overemotional, less reasoned responses ascribed to children. Competence is not therefore a stable attribute of a particular age but rather is a fluid context dependent performance that can be staged by children and adults alike.

Children's Competence in Cyberspace

Many of these debates about children's safety in 'public' space are played out not only in outdoor space, but also in cyberspace. As we enter the Information Age, Information and Communication Technology (ICT) skills are widely understood to be crucial for children's future educational and employment prospects (Valentine, Holloway and Bingham 2002). Yet, at the same time there are popular fears that if children have the technological skills to negotiate cyberspace independently they will be at risk both from dangerous strangers on line, and from being corrupted by the unsuitable materials (e.g. pornography, racial and ethnic hatred, drugs and so on) that can be found on the Internet (Valentine and Holloway 2001). In this way, children are constructed as 'vulnerable' and in need of protection from the adult world in cyberspace, just as they are in outdoor space.

Yet, research suggests that just as children challenge these constructions of their social competence in public space, so too they contest and subvert attempts to manage their access to, and time in, on-line space. In particular, children challenge parents' imagining of an artificial distinction between the sanctuary of the home and the potential dangers and corruption of cyberspace, arguing that there is nothing available on-line that they have not found in magazines, seen on satellite television or heard discussed by their peer groups at school. Just as the boys quoted above use managing risk in outdoor space as a way of negotiating their masculinity, so too using the Internet to surf for pornography and undesirable materials is also an important way for some boys to negotiate their masculinity within the heterosexual economy of the IT classroom (Holloway et al. 2000). Likewise, just as most children are aware of potential stranger-dangers in public space, so too children – particularly girls – are alert to such risks in cyberspace. Again, research suggests that while acknowledging potential risks from on-line contact with disembodied strangers, girls also argue that they are competent and mature enough to take sensible precautions to avoid putting themselves in dangerous situations (Valentine and Holloway 2002). Moreover, in another parallel with the above discussion of outdoor space, many young people also consider their parents to be technologically incompetent (Holloway and Valentine 2001a) and to make unrealistic risk assessments about on-line dangers.

The similarities between the way parents think about children's off-line and on-line safety also extend to the techniques that they employ to restrict and control children's spatial ranges in cyberspace. For example, research suggests that many parents insist that children say which Internet sites they are going to visit; limit the Internet sites where they are allowed to go; insist on surfing the Net with them; and keep a surreptitious eye on children's on-line activities either by locating the PC in a domestic space where they can keep them under surveillance when they are using the Internet or by using the phone bill and on-line records to keep track of where the children have been, when, and for how long (Holloway and Valentine 2001a, 2001b). In a final parallel between on-line and off-line space children also describe various ways that the get round on-line restrictions, that are reminiscent of their tactics for escaping off-line restrictions.

These connections between on-line and off-line worlds offer reciprocal opportunities for children to re-negotiate parents' understandings of their competence in each spatial context. While some children use examples of their social competence in outdoor space to argue that they should be allowed to develop their technological competence by using the Internet unsupervised, other children use their technological competence – which often outstrips that of their parents – as a justification for why they should also be trusted with more autonomy and independence in outdoor space. In this way social and technological competencies co-develop (Valentine and Holloway 2001).

In summary, this chapter has argued that the dominant imagining of childhood in contemporary western societies is one in which children are imagined as 'immature' and incompetent and thus in need of protection by (and from) 'rational', competent adults (see also Chapter One). Through repetitive acts of parenting, which take place within a regulatory framework, and congeal over time, understandings are produced about children's competence (in off-line and on-line spaces) and what it means to be a competent parent, which shape the nature and range of restrictions parents impose on their offspring. These are (re)negotiated in the context of children's own performances of different levels of social and technological competence and their acts of resistance.

Paradoxically, children also perceive their parents to be incompetent in many situations (particularly in relation to risk assessment) and so manage their 'naive' or 'over-emotional' parents in order to extend their personal geographies, often 'protecting' their parents from information which they think they would not be able to 'cope' with. In this way, what it means to be a competent child is intimately bound up with what it means to be a competent parent. These levels of competence are not stable but rather are fluid, shifting and often inconsistent over time and space and between children and parents.

These findings therefore highlight the danger of presuming an adult-child binary in terms of competence, maturity, self awareness and so on and thus in underestimating the abilities of children to manage their own personal safety in off-line and on-line worlds, and overestimating parents capacity as 'guardians'. Rather, 'children are often like adults and adults like children in their rationality, maturity and interdependence' (Alderson and Goodwin 1993: 312). As such we need to recognise that 'adult' and 'child' are unstable and fluid performances; and to consider the radical possibilities that this recognition offers.

Perhaps by breaking away from thinking of children as incompetent, pre-social, less knowledgeable, less able and so on we can begin to re-evaluate children's role in public space and in particular to value children's contribution to, and active participation in, public life. To this end, Chapter Seven reflects on the sort of policies that are required to create and maintain spaces, which are truly accessible to all – not just 'adult' – citizens. But first, Chapter Five considers the impact of parental restrictions (albeit negotiated and contested) on children's use of outdoor space.

Note

1 Schools, the police and the state to some extent also play a part in this process.

Chapter 5

The Retreat from the Street

The previous chapters have focused on parents' risk assessment for their children's safety, identifying a geography of fear in which danger is associated with strangers in public space; and they have examined how, as a consequence, parents negotiate limitations on their children's independent mobility in order to protect them. This chapter explores the consequences of these restrictions. It begins by examining the way that some parents are substituting their children's independent outdoor play with privatised, institutionalised, adult-organised activities such as sports coaching and music lessons, and then goes onto consider why the associated decline in children's public play matters. Finally, it considers inequalities in different children's access to institutional play and independent environmental experiences and reflects on the implications of this. This argument is set within the context of a discussion about economic restructuring and the decline of public space in our cities.

The Privatisation of Children's Play

There is widespread popular concern in both North America and Europe about the future of children's outdoor play. As Chapter Two demonstrated, parental' perceptions that children's opportunity to play in safety has declined since their own youth (McNeish and Roberts 1995) is leading to contemporary children being denied the outdoor play opportunities afforded to previous generations. Notably Chapters Three and Four showed how in response to their fears parents' attempt to limit children's independent use of outdoor space by establishing strict spatial-temporal rules and boundaries that are squeezing young people out of public space (see also Cahill 1990, Blakeley 1994 and Medrich et al. 1982).

However, beyond the crude spatial-temporal rules outlined in the previous chapters, parents also use a range of other techniques to keep children off the streets. Personal computers, video games and other electronic media for example are used by some parents as a positive tool for encouraging children to spend their spare time at home where parents can 'keep an eye on them', even though there have been public scares about the availability of unsuitable material on-line (Holloway and Valentine 2003). Wyness (1994) argues that rather than wanting their children out from under their feet, parents are increasingly opening up their homes to their children's friends in order to have more control over where they are and hence control over their safety.

While overall children's outdoor play is becoming more home centred (and therefore supervised by adults), children are being compensated for the decline in their independent mobility and therefore their independent activity by the substitution of adult-controlled institutional activities (Valentine and McKendrick 1997). Two-thirds of the parents surveyed claimed that their children participate in some form of organised play activities. One-fifth of the respondents stated that their child is a member of at least three different groups. Similarly, in a study of 9–12 year olds in London, UK, Kelley et al. (1998) observed that many children spent a considerable amount of their non-school time in organised, adult-led activities and that few were allowed unsupervised, playing out time. Karsten's (1998) research in the Netherlands, and Dowling's (2000) work in Australia has also documented a similar shift – motivated by concerns about safety – in children's play from public outdoor play to private extra curricula activities, in which children rely on mothers to ferry them from one activity to another.

This public to private shift in children's play has been further promoted by the growth in women's participation in the labour force which has meant that parents have turned to institutionally provided play opportunities as one way of keeping their children safe and out of trouble in the gap between the school day finishing and one of the parents returning home from work (Smith and Barker 2000). Whilst such care was until recently provided by schools in the form of after hours sports training and other semi-educational societies, the recent well documented (Adler and Adler 1994) decline in the provision of these activities has meant that parents now often have to organise these opportunities for their children independently of school.

Indeed, the UK Government has highlighted after school childcare as an important part of a number of major policy initiatives including *Welfare to Work* and the *National Childcare Strategy* (Smith and Barker 1999). As such it has put in place investment to provide up to 30,000 new out-of-school clubs for children. This funding has resulted in the number of such clubs in the UK growing by over 1000 per cent in the decade between the beginning and end of the 1990s (Smith and Barker 2000). Moreover, there has been a general commodification of play with commercial facilities for children – designed to keep them safe within contained environments – increasingly becoming a feature of a whole range of public spaces including: retail outlets, motorway service stations, pubs and restaurants etc. (McKendrick et al. 1999, 2000). Oldman (1994a) uses the term 'childwork' to describe professional childcare that exploits commercial value of children's growth and development in safe environments. Some of these commercial play environments, dubbed 'kid corrals' by Aitken (2001: 153) have been described as shamelessly representing the commodification of parental fears.

As well as protecting children from traffic and stranger-dangers by shielding them from public space, some of these commercial or institutional activities have the added benefit of providing them with play, educational and sporting opportunities outside the home (Adler and Adler 1994). Indeed, parents are increasingly being held responsible for their children reaching their full potential educationally, emotionally and even aesthetically (Beck and Beck-Gernsheim 1995). Individualisation may mean that young people have more choices about how to live their lives, but it is parents who are expected to make considerable material and personal sacrifices to provide their children with the education, equipment, and sports/social activities necessary to make the best start in life (see also Chapter Two). In this sense children often become a 'projection screen' for parents' own unrealised ambitions and desires for social mobility, anchoring their own identities (Beck and Beck-Gernsheim 1995: 138). For middle class adults in particular, whose lives are strongly governed by the dominant time economy, clock time is regarded as a resource to be budgeted, allocated, and controlled (Adam 1995). As such their children's leisure time is increasingly understood as something that should be spent productively in various institutional activities rather than wasted on free play in public space, where there is also a risk that children might 'get in' with the wrong crowd who will undermine the parents' education and undermine their education and employment goals for their offspring. For children in full-time out of school childcare, the vast majority of their waking hours are therefore spent in an institutionalised setting. These parents describe the sort of arrangements they make for their children's leisure time:

> Mother: I take them to various activities e.g. dancing, ballet, tap, gymnastics, swimming and piano lessons ... because we live in such an age where we want our children to do anything and everything and because it's so fast, you know, you all want them to achieve all these things, so all these events all happen together, so it's rush, rush, rush, you must get them here, you must get them back home cos they want to keep up with their peers and everything. And perhaps you should slow down and let them only choose what they want to go to ('middle class', commuter village, Cheshire).

> Father: I mean the majority of things, activities you can make arrangements even though they probably don't like it, making the arrangements for them but at least you can get them to it and bring them home ... Children expect it almost now and we, so that's a way of life ('middle class', rural commuter village, Cheshire).

Indeed, parents' desire to provide private play opportunities for their children are further compounded by the decline in play spaces in public space. Katz (1994, 1998) has drawn particular attention to the way that space set aside for children in the city – parks and playgrounds – is being eroded by disinvestment in community facilities as a result of economic restructuring. This deterioration in the urban environment for US children is summed up for Katz (1994), by the findings of the US Citizen's Budget commission, which classified four out of ten parks and playgrounds in New York City as unsatisfactory.

The vast majority of parents surveyed for this study claimed to be dissatisfied with the public provision of facilities and opportunities for children's play in their neighbourhood. Only 20 per cent of parents considered there were sufficient things for children aged 8–11 to do in their neighbourhood, the figure dropped to seven per cent when the question was asked in relation to children aged 12–15. While the opinion that there is inadequate public provision of play facilities is shared by all social groups, parents who live in 'working class' areas are more likely to consider play opportunities to be inadequate. Some 91 per cent of working class parents expressed this view, compared to 70 per cent of parents in middle class areas (Valentine and McKendrick 1997).

This general picture of dissatisfaction accords with a survey conducted in the UK by MORI for the children's charity Barnardo's which painted an equally bleak picture of children's play spaces in Britain (McNeish and Roberts 1985). Of the 1069 parents who were interviewed as part of this survey, 35 per cent claimed that there was no playground in their neighbourhood and two-thirds of those parents who said there was a playground in their neighbourhood claimed that it was poorly maintained. In a further survey of 94 parents contacted through a range of its play projects, Barnardos also found that parents considered play facilities to be generally poor.

This depressing view of children's outdoor opportunities is not exclusively an urban problem. Ward (1990) argues that contemporary rural children, like their urban counterparts, also have less opportunity to explore their local environment than previous generations. He attributes some of the emptying of young people from the countryside to changes in the rural landscape and land ownership which mean that children are increasingly denied access to fields and open spaces. He further suggests that the contemporary loss of rural hedgerows, ponds, streams and access to woods has had as significant an impact on rural children as it has on wildlife. Yet, there has been a wider policy neglect of the potential difficulties children face in the country (Philo 1997).

Measuring the Impact of Parental Restrictions on Children's Outdoor Play

The growing restrictions on children's outdoor play outlined in the previous section have had a profound impact on children's independent use of space. In a landmark study of children's independent mobility, Hillman, Adams and Whitelegg (1990) compared the freedom children were given to travel independently (e.g. to go to school unaccompanied by an adult) in 1971 with the experiences of children in 1990. The study mapped a drastic decline in children's personal freedom. For example, in 1971 their survey found that 80 per cent of seven to eight year old children were permitted to go to school on their own, but by 1990 this figure had plunged to a mere nine per cent.

Similarly, the median age at which children were granted 'licences' (their term for the freedom to make non school journeys involving catching a bus or crossing the road without an adult) had risen by over two and a half years. Between 1971–90 they recorded a drop of over 50 per cent in the number of children allowed to go places other than school on their own, while the number of cycle owning primary school aged children allowed to ride on the roads had fallen from two-thirds to just a quarter. Thus they concluded that '[t]he personal freedom and choice permitted a typical seven year old in 1971 are now not permitted until children reach the age of about nine and half' (Hillman et al 1990: 106).

Other measures used to estimate the extent of children's spatial independence include Newson and Newson's (1976) use of summary measures to classify children as either indoor or outdoor children; and Moore's documentation of children's favoured play locations. Taken against these studies, the survey conducted as part of this research has observed a marked reduction in children's independent use of outdoor space that parallels Hillman et al.'s (1990) measure of children's declining independent mobility. Significantly fewer children are now considered outdoor children (23 per cent) compared to when Newson and Newson (1976) conducted their research two decades ago (when 60 per cent of children were described as outdoor children, by the age of seven). Likewise, most contemporary 'outdoor play' is now closely centred on the home and its immediate environs, a findings that contrasts with Moore's study, which found that home sites were the favoured place for only 20 per cent of children's play. While it was often difficult for parents to ascribe one particular play site as the dominant location of children's play around 40 per cent of parents responding to the survey said that their children spend most of their outdoor leisure time in private gardens. In other words, a significant amount of children's outdoor play is taking place in 'private' space, rather than 'public' space, so that although children are spending a considerable proportion of their leisure time 'outdoors' most have very limited opportunities to play in, or to explore the public environment independently of adult supervision. This tallies with the Barnardo's survey which found that most children play in their garden or yard and that 44 per cent of children never or hardly ever played outdoors without adult supervision (McNeish and Roberts 1995).

Perhaps the extent, and the significance, of children in western societies' inhibited geographies has been most effectively demonstrated through the work of Katz (1998). In a study of girls' use of outdoor space in New York, US, Katz (1998) found that the independent mobility of young women who participated in her research was constrained by fear of crime and disinvestments in the urban environment. She then related these experiences to other research she had conducted with young women in the Islamic culture of Howa, Sudan where girls are constrained by Purdah. Strikingly, Katz (1998) concluded that the girls in New York, the ultimate contemporary western society, may be more restricted in their ability to explore and engage with their own local environment than girls in what westerners would consider a more restrictive culture such as Islamic Sudan.

Why the Decline in Children's Independent Use of Space Matters

This decline in children's independent mobility and use of space in contemporary western societies matters because play is a means through which children's physical, mental and creative capabilities are developed. This point is not lost on the international community who recognise that play is one of the fundamental rights of the child, alongside more familiar concerns such as protection from exploitation, abuse and neglect, and provision of health and education services (see also Chapter Seven). Formal recognition of this right is expressed through Article 38 of 'The United Nations (UN) Convention on the Rights of the Child' (hereafter 'the convention') which was adopted by the UN General Assembly on 20th November 1989 and ratified by countries, spanning every continent and harbouring a rich diversity of cultures (Rosenbaum 1993). The convention directs those governments who ratify the treaty to promote and improve children's play experiences. It states that: 'State parties recognise the right of the child to rest and leisure, to engage in play and recreational activities appropriate to the age of the child … and shall encourage the provision of appropriate and equal opportunities for … recreational and leisure activity' (UN, Article 38: 2).

Outdoor play in particular is crucial because it is the primary mechanism through which children become acquainted with their environment. For example, the freedom to play and move freely in the environment is one of the means by which children develop 'natural' mapping skills (Blaut 1971, Blaut and Stea 1974). Children's spatial knowledge and competency grows as their geographies expand from home to garden, to neighbourhood and the wider city. Buchner (1990) argues however, that by ferrying children to and from institutional activities, parents are robbing children of the opportunity to develop their own understanding of their local environment and giving them a dislocated sense of space. Describing children's everyday journeys from one activity to another he writes: '[t]he spaces in between rush past and are often perceived only superficially, with the result that a child's subjective map becomes a patchwork carpet consisting of islands of apparently unconnected space' (Buchner 1990: 79). Moreover, most commercial playgrounds (a term that encompasses a whole range of play spaces and genres including specialist leisure facilities and add-on playspaces to places such as retail outlets etc.) are predominantly situated indoors, and so serve to limit children's use of the environment to these specially designated spaces (McKendrick et al. 2000). The amount of time that children spend indoors has been put forward as one possible explanation for why recent research has shown that UK children are becoming more obese.

Many of the institutionalised activities provided for UK children, such as after school clubs – though privately run – are held in the space of the school. Children's ability to use, and transform these environments or even to access particular pieces of equipment or places to play is therefore usually limited by institutional rules and the practices/demands of the school (Smith and Barker 2000). Smith and Barker (2000: 246) observe that '[T]he institutionalised environment of the out of school club therefore represents another place in the social and cultural landscape of childhood where adults try to shape children's use of space ...'. Moreover, because after-school clubs are only transient occupants of school buildings they are sometimes forced to move location to accommodate other institutional needs. These are processes over which the clubs have little control, and the children none at all.

Having time on their own is important for children in developing and contributing to their experience of independence (Solberg 1990). Yet, the institutionalisation of children's play also means that children's use of time, like their use of space, is being increasingly structured around adults' lives (Oldman 1994b). It gives adults – including parents, teachers and care workers – a greater say in who children spend their leisure time with. This has led Buchner (1990: 79) to bemoan the fact that: '[c]hildren's street world, formed relatively independently [from adults] and composed of children from a variety of backgrounds and age groups, is increasingly being replaced by integration into various peer-group social sets, often chosen and supervised by parents for particular purposes and activities'.

Institutional play is characterised by being organised, competitive, and routinised. It is usually adults who establish the rules and regulations and who take responsibility for decision making (Nasman 1994, Smith and Barker 2000). According to Adler and Adler (1994) institutionalized play is therefore hierarchical and serious, rather than spontaneous and carefree, and so denies children the sort of opportunities to develop self-reliance, co-operation, problem solving and interpersonal skills which more spontaneous independent play is credited with teaching them (although it is important to recognise that children do contest and attempt to redefine and reclaim institutional spaces from their adult caretakers – Smith and Barker 2000).

While adults emphasise the benefits of safe playgrounds and institutional play spaces, children need places which afford different kinds of opportunities and experiences (Gibson 1979). Indeed, there is some evidence that children do not necessarily want the sort of institutional or indoor play opportunities that they are being given, and that adults fail to take into account children's ways of seeing (Matthews 1995). Writers such as Ward (1978) and Sibley (1991) suggest that there is often a mismatch between play provision for children and what children actually want. Notably, children often prefer to play in diverse and 'flexible' landscapes (in terms of surfaces, forms, materials, opportunities for creative and manipulative play etc.), such as waste ground and open spaces, rather than playgrounds and other formally designated and provided play sites. Indeed derelict and disordered spaces are pivotal in children's books as spaces that children appropriate (Jones 1997). In a cross-national study in the UK and US, Moore found that open spaces/ outdoors was the most favoured play site for children aged between eight and thirteen. He describes children's 'patterns of interaction' with environments as being 'more intimate, fluid and intense' than those of adults (Moore 1986: 57); while studies by Hart (1979) and Wood (1985a, 1985b) have both observed the amount of time children spend playing in the dirt or the snow, building tree houses and constructing their own dens and secret places. Children equally enjoy creating differently striated space in the countryside as well as urban neighbourhoods (Jones 2000). Indeed, one of the very attractions of outdoor play for children is the possibilities that it offers them to appropriate public space (space which is normally taken for granted as an adult space) in imaginative ways for themselves. Aitken and Ginsberg (1988) have observed the way children are at adept at turning everything from ornamental ponds to walls, into skateboard runs, while Hart (1979) has noted the way that children often give their favourite places names which reflect the way they use them – 'sliding hill' for example. In such ways, then, children make themselves 'at home' in public space. In a classic study of children's games and folklore, Opie and Opie (1969: 15) argue that the 'peaks of a child's experience are ... occasions when he [sic] escapes into places that are disused and overgrown and silent'.

These sorts of places where children exercise their creativity and imagination have a social role too, in that they can provide young people with the privacy to experiment with their identities and develop their own notions of morality and empathy (Aitken 2001). Winnicott's notion of transitional space, particularly the 'space of play', focuses on flexible environments where meanings are open to manipulation, as key qualities of play that shape how the self develops. Transitional space is a safe place for experimentation because it lies beyond society's rules, and as such is a space from where society's rules can be challenged by children (Aitken 2001). This understanding of the potential role of outdoor play is evident in this mother's description of what her children are missing out on because of her fears for their safety:

> Mother: I mean I think it would be lovely to be able to let them go out and play in the woods you know, because they would learn so much, they would grow. You know they don't, they don't grow the same, they can't, they don't learn responsibility because they can't and they don't have the ability to go out themselves and learn to get themselves out of difficulties ... like skating on the pond or playing over in the weirs ('middle class', commuter village, Cheshire).

A number of studies have suggested that as a result of children's retreat from the street, and the institutionalisation of children's leisure time, these sorts of play opportunities – dubbed by Aitken 'thick play' are in decline. Aitken (2001: 177) writes such '[t]ransitional spaces of unmitigated potential, creativity and imagination are diminishing because they are threatening to adult control and comfort zones'. Some parents interviewed as part of this study even went so far as to argue that because their children do not have the opportunity to engage in imaginative independent play they are losing the ability to amuse themselves. This change was lamented by many parents, who contrasted their own childhood memories of playing freely outdoors and taking over the streets with their children's more spatially restricted and controlled upbringings.

> Mother: Oh golly, I lived in the middle of a town and we'd got a big park where I lived and there's lots of woods and a river on this park – I could go all over that park at Katy's age. I would go down to the river, play on ropes and swings, I'd go all over the place and it was full of all sorts of people but it just didn't seem to be a problem then. If I lived there now I wouldn't let Katy do it. She couldn't do what I did as a child ('middle class', non-metropolitan town, Cheshire).

> Mother: I mean you do remember your own childhood and I remember mine. Mine was, you know, it was lovely being able to play outside and I went, um, a lot further afield than what I allow my children to do, you know really when I think about it now, it even frightens meself ... You know being able to play out until dark in the summer. There is just something exciting about that somehow, you know it is really good. I mean you know I used to live in the village next to this one and I mean we used to go for a picnic way, way out of the village in the woods, and it was lovely you know. But if Cody said I'm going to the woods with a friend, you know, you would say 'no you're not', you know. I don't think even I'd walk to the woods on me own now, so, um, you know the boundary's come in a lot ('middle class', rural area, Derbyshire).

> Mother: Sometimes you can say 'just go and play' and they say 'what shall I do?' They can't always just amuse themselves, you sometimes feel they've got to be amused ... if they haven't got something handed to them on a plate all the time, they just don't know how to play ('middle class', rural area, Derbyshire).

This is not to suggest however, that previous generations were given complete freedom to explore outdoors by their parents. There is a danger that many accounts of past childhoods are romanticised or over stated. Indeed, two-thirds of the parents recalled in the questionnaire survey that they were restricted by play rules as a child. But despite the inherent difficulties of mapping the past it is important to consider the changing patterns of outdoor play because remembered childhoods (when children played freely outdoors) whether 'real' or 'imagined' are used as a vehicle for expressing concern with contemporary childhood (the lack of outdoor play) and, indeed, are to some extent a root cause of this concern (changing play patterns).

However, this research provided limited opportunities to explore the reasons why patterns of outdoor play have changed between generations as background data on historical circumstances is understandably incomplete. Two distinct eras can be identified in which the extent of outdoor play has changed. First, the sharply differing assessments of parents aged over 45 (82 per cent of whom recollect that they played outdoors more often than their child), with those aged 40–44 (58 per cent of whom recollect more outdoor play), suggest that significant changes in patterns of play were evident in the late fifties/early sixties (when these parents were the same age as their children). Second, the comparability of recollections of parents currently in their twenties, early thirties, late thirties and forties – 61 per cent, 59 per cent, 57 per cent and 58 per cent of whom recollect more outdoor play than their child – suggest that there was a subsequent period of stability (when these parents were children), which has since been followed by a more drastic reduction in outdoor play in the last ten to twenty years (since those parents in their twenties were children). These results dispute the notion of a constant reduction in children's outdoor play and raise the need for historians of childhood to look more closely at the contemporary history of children's lives.

Although we were all children once, some writers argue that it is difficult to do this by relying on adult accounts of growing up because our memories of this period are flawed and we can never really re-enter the world of childhood (Aitken and Herman 1997). However, Philo (2003) suggests that things like the undirected drawings, jottings, diaries and stories, we produced as children are important secondary sources that might be used to shed light on our early worlds – particularly the imaginations and reveries of our childhood.

Unequal Opportunities to Play

While this chapter has described a striking pattern in the decline in children's independent mobility and use of outdoor space, it is also true that the restrictions being imposed on children are not uniform. Studies suggest that 'working class' children's activities and use of space are subject to less supervision by adults than middle class children (Mercer 1976). For example, a Barnardos' study concluded that children from low income families and deprived neighbourhoods are less likely to enjoy relatively safe and exciting play opportunities than children from middle class backgrounds (McNeish and Roberts 1995). Karsten (1998) observed a similar pattern in the Netherlands, where she found that middle class children and children from white Dutch families had more opportunities to participate in clubs and organised play activities than children from poorer backgrounds and children from Turkish, Moroccan and Surinamese/Antillean backgrounds.

Likewise, the evidence of this research is that the outdoor play of children who live in rented accommodation (64 per cent) is less likely to be home-based compared to those who live in owner-occupied accommodation (77 per cent); while children who live in predominately working class areas or mixed class areas (84 per cent) are more likely to be described as outdoor children compared to children living in middle class areas (74 per cent). Indeed, while a clear majority of children spend most of their play time in home-based locations, there are particular locales where home-based play is a minority experience. While the outdoor play of 87 per cent of children from Hunters Bridge (a middle class commuter village) could be described as home-based, in Shenford (a mixed class urban metropolitan area) 57 per cent of children spend most of their play time beyond the immediate vicinity of the home.

Moreover the research found that children of lone parents are the most 'outdoor' children and play most frequently beyond the immediate vicinity of their homes. While many lone parents want to supervise their children's play in the same way as two parent households, the reality of managing alone is that lone parents often have to allow their children more spatial freedom than other children are permitted because they do not have a partner to share the physical, emotional and financial burden of supervising their offspring with (see also Chapter Three).

Just as middle class caregivers can often afford childcare and private play schemes in the city, so too in rural areas, safe play space is also a class privilege (Aitken 1994, Katz 1993, Valentine 1997c). Indeed some of the parents in Wheldale, a Derbyshire village, had purchased their own land specifically to reproduce all the ingredients of a purified, innocent, organic rural childhood for their children, and their friends, in a way denied those without similar financial resources. These parents explain the opportunities they are able to provide their children with:

Mother: We've got four acres up there and they can do what they like in it because it is completely private, you can't get into it apart from through our gate, two gates actually, so it is not somewhere that someone is going to wander into ('middle class', rural village, Derbyshire).

Mother: I wouldn't let my kids play in the fields round here. There is a family, the Smethurst's [referring to the woman quoted above] who've got three fields and the kids go up into their fields but they [the Smethurst children] know their own fields. And they [her own children] know Sally [another villager] up there, they've bought a field too, probably for a very similar reason, you know, a safe area ... And I've actually started to teach my children, I know its sounds really funny, how to play, which sounds really strange ... I've actually started to teach them imaginative play. They make dens and stuff (middle class, rural village, Derbyshire).

Father: They don't even play down in the village you see, so they only play in our garden and on our land ('middle class', rural village, Derbyshire).

There are two paradoxical consequences of these patterns. On the one hand, children from middle-class urban areas (80 per cent) are more likely to participate in organised play than those from low income areas (60 per cent) (reflecting middle class parents' superior income and mobility) and therefore are likely to benefit from educational and social opportunities that will enable them to reproduce their class position as adults. Notably, Adler and Adler claim (1994: 325) that: 'If these experiences [of institutionalised play] prepare youngsters for the corporate work world – partly through their enhanced "cultural capital" of additional knowledge, skills and disposition and partly through the "habitus", the attitude and experience of achievement they acquire – then after school activities are yet another route to reproducing social inequalities' (Adler and Adler 1994: 325).

On the other hand, however, while the more heavily chaperoned 'middle class' children are usually perceived to have the better (i.e. more privatised) play opportunities, it is the children from lone parent households whose play is more independent and 'public' focused, and who therefore may well have the richest environmental experiences. This is evident in a cross cultural study by Lynch (1979) that found that children in some of the poorest neighbourhoods actually had some of the most valuable and varied experiences of their local environment, creating their own rich microcultures and geographies out of stark and harsh landscapes.

In this way local geographies matter, both in terms of the material conditions/characteristics of the neighbourhoods where children live and the social and cultural relations produced within them. While similar processes (such as fear of crime, the commodification of children's play, disinvestment in the environment etc.) are evident in all the research sites, these are refracted differently within the different localities (in terms of localised discourses and practices of 'good' parenting, the role of the 'community' and other resources available so on) to reproduce subtly different experiences and expectations. In this way, the specificity of place produces and is produced by the distinct juxtapositions and convergence of wider and local social relations (Massey 1993).

Battery-Reared Children: The Implications for Public Space

The sort of constriction of children's access to independent leisure time in public space, that has been described in this chapter, has led a *Sunday Times* journalist to claim that '[T]hese days our children are not so much free-ranged as battery-reared' (cited in McNeish and Roberts 1995: 3). This has important implications for the way that public space is being produced. Concern about children's safety is resulting in children being pushed into privatised spaces – the home, or institutional venues such as after school clubs or leisure centres – for their own protection. This retreat of children from the street is facilitating the appearance that public space is 'naturally' or 'normally' an adult space (of course public space is also produced as adult space in many other ways, for example through laws that define the age at which a person can drive a car, go into a bar serving alcohol and so on). In other words, that it is a space where unaccompanied young children are 'out of place' (see also Chapters Two and Six).

Yet, independent outdoor play in public space is a vital means through which children develop physically, mentally and socially. Despite the UN's recognition of its importance (see also Chapter Seven) it remains a low priority issue for the UK Government and local authorities. Family status emerges as one of the most important mediators of experience. This is an important contribution to knowledge as geographers have tended to overlook this factor in their accounts of children's play and, more generally, the late twentieth and early twenty-first centuries have been characterised by increasing diversity of family forms. Children of lone parents experience more of the local neighbourhood (more are 'outdoor' children, more play beyond the immediate vicinity of the home), while lone parents themselves are more dissatisfied with local play provision because they have less resources to provide alternative 'private' opportunities for their children. While this 'public' focus permits a richer environmental experience for pre-adolescent children from lone parent families, than that experienced by children from more 'privatised' families, these children are missing out on the enhanced 'cultural capital' acquired by 'middle class' children when they participate in institutional activities.

The level of parental anxiety about children's safety in public space and the growth in home-based and institutional play outlined in this chapter raises many doubts for those public institutions concerned with providing opportunities for children's play over the utility of the provision of neighbourhood public play facilities. This is not to argue for a *laissez-faire* style 'policy' of non-intervention. On the contrary, the primary political objective needs to be to tackle parents fears about children's safety in public space so the shackles of parental regulation might be relaxed and the opportunities imbedded in every local environment can be realised by children themselves through independent exploration. Aitken (2001: 176) sums this up nicely when he writes: 'Play is the active exploration of individual and social imaginaries, built up in the spaces of everyday life. The challenge around children's rights is to develop legal structures that are robust enough to protect the notion of *thick* play [itals in the original], but flexible enough to guard against its objectification and commodification.' He further continues: 'giving young people space is more than giving them room to play, it is giving them the opportunity for unchallenged and critical reflection on experiences' (Aitken 2001: 180).

Chapter 6

Contested Terrain:
Teenagers in Public Space

While the previous chapters have argued that adults produce public space as an environment that young children are too incompetent or too vulnerable to negotiate alone, their spatial hegemony is more openly contested by teenagers struggling to assert their independence. Hanging around on street corners and larking about in public space become (deliberately and unintentionally) a form of resistance to adult power. A strategy of resistance that is often read as a threat to the safety of young children, adults and to the peace and order of the street. This chapter therefore switches the book's focus of attention from pre-adolescent children to young people. It begins by exploring the contemporary 'othering' of teenagers. It then goes on to consider how a moral panic about 'dangerous' youth has led to popular claims that liberal approaches to children's welfare and children's rights have eroded young people's deference to adults, so undermining the subtle regulatory regimes by which adults maintain their hegemony in public space. The chapter concludes by showing how these arguments in turn have been used to win consensus for spatial and temporal restrictions on, and tighter surveillance and policing of, young people's activities in an attempt to (re)draw the boundaries between adults and children in public space.

Nowhere to Go, Nothing to Do: Teenagers' Experiences of Public Space

Children and teenagers have little privacy[1] relative to adults. At home or school they are subject to the gaze of teachers, siblings and relatives who often try to channel them into organised activities (see Chapter Five) that conflict with their own agendas (Qvortrup 1994). Home, in particular, is a space that is constituted through a complex range of familial rules and regulations (Wood and Beck 1990, 1994) and, as such, boundary disputes with parents are commonplace (Sibley 1995). In particular, Sibley (1995) suggests that domestic tensions around home rules and the use of different rooms within the family home represent a conflict between adults' desire to establish order, regularity and strong domestic boundaries, and young people's preferences for disorder and weak boundaries. Like, the home, the school is also a highly regulated institution with its clearly de-limited boundaries and moral geographies (Fielding 2000). This girl describes her lack of freedom:

Girl: Cos like you're parents don't let you have a lot of freedom and like school's always nagging at you to do things, like when they're talking to you they talk to you as a little child not an adult ('working class', metropolitan area, Yorkshire).

As the previous chapter has argued, there is little public (as opposed to private) provision of facilities for young people in UK towns and cities, let alone the countryside. Moreover, teenagers commonly want to participate in adult activities rather than be corralled with young children in specialist environments. Public space is therefore an important arena for young people wanting to escape adult surveillance and define their own identities and ways of being. However, efforts to revitalize or 'aestheticise' public space as part of attempts to revive (symbolically and economically) cities in most contemporary western cities are increasingly resulting in the replacement of 'public' spaces with surrogate 'private' spaces such as shopping malls and festival marketplaces. The development of these new privatised spaces of consumption, and broader processes of gentrification, are serving to homogenise and domesticate public spaces by reducing and controlling diversity in order to make these environments safe for the middle classes (Smith 1992, Fyfe and Bannister 1998). It is a process which has been termed the disneyfying (Sorkin 1992) or annihilation (Mitchell 1996) of public space. Among the undesirable 'others' being priced out, or driven out of these commercial social, retail and leisure complexes by the private security industries (including guards and closed circuit television – CCTV – surveillance) are teenagers. Norris and Armstrong's (1997, cited in Graham 1998) ethnographic study of CCTV control rooms for example, uncovered the way that certain types of young people are labelled 'yobs', 'toe-rags' or 'drug-dealing scrotes' by operators who impose a normative space-time ecology on the environments they manage, removing all those who they determine to be unwelcome. Such processes hide the extent to which the public realm is being privatised and commodified and reinforce the importance of the street for contemporary young people (Vanderbeck and Johnson 2000, Skelton 2000).

Notably, the space of the neighbourhood or city street, particularly after dark, when many adults have retreated to the sanctuary of the home, is often the only autonomous space many teenagers are able to carve out for themselves, and is therefore an important social arena where young people can be together (Corrigan 1979, Skelton 2000). With nothing particular to do, young people often roam the streets looking for excitement because the street can be a place where special things happen (Lieberg 1995). Moreover, the very act of doing nothing is in Woods (1985a) terms doing something because it is a time when children have the freedom and privacy from adult supervision to be themselves. This is increasingly important to young people given the fact that doing nothing is becoming less and less possible for children in the culture of contemporary parenting in which children are ferried from one institutional activity to another (see Chapter Five). These young people explain:

Girl 1: For lots of things there is restrictions on for teenagers, like we're not allowed to go places and do things.
Girl 2: It's boring, that's when we hang on street corners. We keep together.

Boy 1: We go out everyday.
Boy 2: So we're always out somewhere.
Boy 1: We'll be out till about ten o'clock.
Boy 2: Just hanging about.
Boy 1: I used to go to the caf[e]. There's a pool table there but now it stinks.
Boy 2: Because people in there smoke you see it gets in your clothes and you get caught (group discussion, 'working class', metropolitan area, Yorkshire).

Hanging around on street corners, in parks, underage drinking, petty vandalism and larking about and other forms of non-adherence to order on the street become (deliberately and unconsciously) a form of resistance to adult power. Spencer et al. (1989: 230) use the term 'alternative scripts' to describe the way teenagers occupy and use public space differently from adults. Groups or gangs of young people – finely delineated by age – often colonise and contest control of particular spaces, such as bus-shelters, parks, as their own. They stake a claim on these spaces both by their physical presence, and by marking their territory or ownership with graffiti (Ley and Cybriwsky 1974) or other markers like rubbish. Different groups of young people use these places to play out identity struggles, excluding each other from 'their territory' through name calling, bullying and general antagonism and intimidation (Percy-Smith and Matthews 2001, Tucker and Matthews 2001). Girls' single sex friendship groups are especially marginalised through such tactics by older mixed groups (Tucker 2003).

Girl 1: We hang around outside with our friends.
Girl 2: You feel safer hanging around with a gang of people.
Girl 4: More people you know.
Girl 2: Yeah in your own area.
Interviewer: Do you ever have any frightening experiences?
Girl 3: Yeah sometimes.
Girl 1: When they [other groups of teenagers] come up and start swearing and ...
Girl 3: Bullying ya, and saying things to ya (group discussion, 'working class', metropolitan area, Yorkshire).

Over the recent past the public realm, rather than being a social order of civility, sociability and tolerance, has increasingly become one of apprehension and insecurity. Encounters with 'difference' are being read not as pleasurable and part of the vitality of the streets but rather as potentially threatening and dangerous (Mitchell 1996, Zukin 1995). In this context, young people's nonconformity and disorderly behaviour is often read as a threat to the personal safety of other children and the elderly and as threat to the peace and order of the street. The fear that their children may come to harm at the hands of other violent children was particularly, though not exclusively, expressed by interviewees in relation to boys and was the justification some parents gave for restricting their sons' use of space (see also Chapter Three). These parents explain their concerns:

> Mother: [T]hat's not something I particularly fear of, not abduction, I think I'd be more frightened, more concerned that he might may be caught up by a group of lads who would really beat him up and really hurt him, not just come home crying but you know head butt him and all the rest of it ('working class', metropolitan area, Greater Manchester).

> Mother: Our Daniel went to the Civic on Saturday to do some shopping. And there were these three lads – about 15 they were. And he could tell that they were about to start on him so he stayed on the bus – he got off and got back on and stayed on till Portway Road cos he said he knew they were gonna go for him … He said … they were gonna start on him cos they was just looking at him ('working class', metropolitan area, Greater Manchester).

> Father: … it's not the perverts who are going to snatch them off because frankly that's so slight a chance it's virtually never going to happen, it's the teenage oiks.
> Mother: Yeah I mean the other evening, early, the eldest one went across [to the park] with a group of friends and she had stones thrown at her.
> Father: In fact the park … we went we took the bikes, didn't we, and the kids went through the entrance cos it's one of those staggered things you know, you've got to get off your bike. And we all got off the bikes and they got on and off they went and some kids there gave her a right mouthful didn't they [swearing at their daughter].
> Mother: They were having a bit of a go at them because they thought they were on their own ('middle class', non-metropolitan area, Cheshire).

Young people are not only considered 'out of place' on urban streets, they are an equal cause of concern in rural areas as these quotes suggest:

> Mother: There is a problem with teenage children hanging around. They are hanging around at the moment, well they've been there for a while now at the bottom of the school drive, in cars … It is really off putting because the cubs meet there and, um, they were frightened you know. Even I was a bit, when I used to walk down and meet Robbie when it was dark, you know, just walking past these cars, it was a bit spooky ('middle class', rural area, Derbyshire).

> Mother: We had an incident last summer while we were away on holiday, we came back to hear that there had been gangs of youths around the village in fast cars, you know, they thought it was drugs and all this sort of thing. Then we started cubs again and I was a bit worried because the lads coming into cubs, especially the younger ones were very intimidated … So I contacted the police and they came down. They said well they're not doing anything, they are just meeting their friends and we know the lads so we don't think drugs are involved. I said 'right, if they're innocent tell them to come in'. And when the lads [the cubs] saw them they realised they actually knew some of them … and it took all the myth out of

it so they weren't afraid anymore. So we haven't had any problems with town teenagers. These were all ones from the local villages coming in to meet the girls which is fair enough, they have got to have somewhere to go because there is nothing else for them to do here ('middle class', rural area, Derbyshire).

As some of the quotes above indicate, the threat posed by 'dangerous children' is also experienced by many mothers for their own safety. Women described feeling intimidated by groups of teenagers on the streets; some even adopt precautionary measures such as crossing the road, or changing their route in order to avoid putting themselves in places where they feel at risk of teenager violence. There appears to be a different geography of women's fear in each of the neighbourhoods where the research was carried out because the gangs of young people colonise different spaces in each area. For example, in one village they were associated with the bus stop on the high street, in a city neighbourhood they were perceived to have appropriated an area near a derelict pub and in one of the non-metropolitan areas they congregated on a parade of shops, whereas in another similar area, a park was identified as their territory. These women describe their concerns:

Mother: I've seen a um, standing with cans of lager outside the shop. Now I'm not saying that we didn't sort of buy a bottle of Strongbow cider or something but we wouldn't ever do it blatantly in front of adults like that outside a shop ... they're a lot less frightened of authority than we were, we'd never have done certain things that they do, I'm sure of that ... I tend to keep away from them because I find them threatening myself when they're all in a big group and like I say they don't have much respect for authority or older people ('middle class', non-metropolitan area, Cheshire).

Mother: ... when I've gone down to the park and they're all hanging around I find it really intimidating and to be, to feel like that about kids, really it not nice ... they didn't look much older than 13 or 12 ('middle class', non-metropolitan area, Derbyshire).

Yet most research suggests that teenagers hanging around on the street do not deliberately set out to intimidate women, the elderly and other children in public space, nor do they intend to cause trouble. Rather posturing and larking around sometimes leads to laws being broken or to children disrupting adults' worlds but that this is not usually premeditated but is a by-product of natural flows of activities (Corrigan 1979). Rather young people criticise the lack of public space available to them and unreasonable intervention of adults into their social worlds (Corrigan 1979). These teenagers from an urban metropolitan area in Greater Manchester commented:

If the youth club were open there wouldn't be no big gangs outside cos we'd be in the youth club. They wouldn't have to moan at us about smokin', drinkin' and shop liftin', or whatever, if the youth club were open. There's nothing else for us to do.

We're not going round smashing things up. It's cos we've got nothing to do that we hang round here … Every teenager does it.

Despite young people's innocent intentions, their very presence in public places is often considered not only frightening but also a potential threat to public order. Cahill (1990: 399) suggests that:

> [w]hile adults treat younger children in public places as innocent, endearing yet sometimes exasperating incompetents, they treat older children as unengaging and frightfully undisciplined rogues. Among other things, the very violations of public etiquette that adults often find amusing when committed by younger children are treated as dangerous moral failings when the transgressor is a few years older.

The suburbs in particular, have a certain moral order based on an over-whelmingly powerful and widely understood pattern of restraint and non confrontation (Baumgartner 1988). Residents have established 'norms' or appropriate ways of behaving towards each other and often have little contact with 'other' groups who are regarded as unpredictable and threatening. As such, adults regard teenagers, as a menace to the moral order of neighbour-hoods because of the way they are perceived to threaten property through acts of vandalism but more importantly adults' peace and tranquillity – what Cahill (2000) terms the 'rules of the neighbourhood'. These quotes illustrate some of the way adults regard young people as bringing disorder to the streets:

> Mother: … they congregate round the Western shop area, round there then they move along for so many weeks and they were down on Thornton Square near the shops down there, they just seem to congregate. We had a spate where they were just coming up and ripping up 'For Sale' signs just for sheer devilment … At the moment they've got a new game which as a crowd they're running up and down here, knocking on people's doors, ringing the bells and generally being a nuisance ('middle class', non-metropolitan area, Cheshire).

> Father: We have trouble at the back, with teenagers on the back there, only kids, vandalism more than anything. I've been out to try and stop them but it doesn't make any difference ('middle class', metropolitan area, Greater Manchester).

While several interviewees recalled that they too spent their own childhoods hanging around the streets in gangs, tormenting adults in their neighbourhoods, these actions were painted as innocent pranks. In contrast they interpret similar behaviour by contemporary young people as signifying that teenagers are aggressive, intimidating and out of control in public space (even though there appears to be little, aside from anecdotal, evidence of any actual increase in teenage violence). This line of argument is typified by this quote:

Mother: I mean we used to do it when we were young, we'd just hang round at the Mission there. But we wasn't there to cause trouble, we were just there because we liked each others' company, we didn't fight and cause trouble like they do … We were no angels, don't get me wrong, but we weren't violent like they are now … I mean like where I used to live [in a house near a location where the teenagers now congregate] you just couldn't control these kids, [if you told them off] they'd pick up wood or bricks, whatever they'd got in their hands and just throw it at you ('working class', metropolitan area, Greater Manchester).

The notion of a 'moral panic' – 'invented' by the sociologist Stanley Cohen to explain the public outcry caused by the clashes between 'mods' and 'rockers' in England in the mid 1960s – is a useful concept for thinking about how various youth cultures and young people's behaviour in general is often viewed by adultist society as 'criminal' or 'deviant'. Cohen (1972: 9) defines a moral panic thus:

A condition, episode, person or group of persons emerges to become defined as a threat to societal values and interests; its nature presented in a stylized and stereotypical fashion by the mass media, the moral barricades are manned by editors, bishops, politicians and other right-thinking people; socially accredited experts pronounce their diagnoses and solutions; ways of coping are evolved or (more often) resorted to; the condition then disappears, submerges or deteriorates and becomes more visible.

The media play a pivotal role in moral panics by representing a deviant group or event and their effects in an exaggerated way. They begin with warnings of an approaching social catastrophe. When an appropriate event happens which symbolises that this catastrophe has occurred, the media paint what is often a sensational and distorted picture of what has happened in which certain details are given symbolic meanings. In turn the media then provide a forum for the reaction to, and interpretation of, what has taken place. The public then become more sensitive to the issue raised which means that similar 'deviations', which may otherwise have passed unnoticed, also receive a lot of publicity. This spiral of anxiety can eventually lead to punitive action being taken against the 'deviant' group or event by relevant authorities. In this sense McRobbie (1994) suggests that moral panics are about instilling fear into people. Fear either to encourage them to turn away from complex social problems or more commonly fear in order to orchestrate consent for 'something to be done' by the dominant social order.

Moral panics are related to conflicts of interest and discourses of power and are often associated with particular 'symbolic locations' such as the street. These panics are frequently mobilised in relation to particular groups of young people, such as mods and rockers, when they appear to be taking over the streets or threatening the moral order of the suburbs. In this sense McRobbie (1994) argues that moral panics are increasingly less about social control and more about a fear of being out of control and an attempt to discipline the young. This process often involves nostalgia for a mythical 'golden age' where social stability and strong moral discipline were a deterrent to disorder and delinquency. Indeed, Boethius (1995) even goes so far as to suggest that by criticising the young and their lifestyle, adults defend their own more disciplined way of living and try to convince themselves that by becoming adults they have not lost anything. Such moral panics have been evident in both the US and UK at the end of the twentieth and beginning of the twenty-first centuries.

Across the US, young people are currently the subject of popular suspicion and anxiety. One of the key triggers of this contemporary concern is the perceived omni-presence of youth gangs on the street, in which 'gang' has become a code-word for 'race' and a symbol too of drugs, guns, graffiti, gangsta rap and violence (Lucas 1998). The media have played a key role here in exaggerating the number of gangs and in distorting their activities through racialised constructions of youth violence. While violence is presented as a black problem 'one of the terrifying visions of white suburbanites is that of the migration of drive-by-shooting gang bangers ... to the more prosperous (white) peripheral neighbourhoods' (Dumm 1994: 185). In this sense, moral panics about youth gangs are indicative of more general processes of social polarisation. As a result the issue has become increasingly politicised resulting in the inclusion of measures to prosecute gangs members and treat juveniles as adults in the *Violent Crime Control and Law Enforcement Act* of 1994 (Lucas 1998).

Over the last decade over one thousand US cities and smaller communities have introduced curfews on teenagers which require young people aged under 17 years old to be off the streets by 10.30–11pm (The Office of Juvenile Justice and Delinquency Prevention 1996). Over seventy cities have even gone so far as bring in day time curfews too (Riechmann 1997). Such juvenile curfew ordinances have a long history. They were first popular in North America in the late nineteenth century when they were introduced to calm middle-class fears about the need to control working class and immigrant children/neighbourhoods (Lester 1996). Commenting on the introduction of similar curfews in New Zealand, Collins and Kearns (2001) argue that curfews are disciplinary mechanisms that work on the principle of the panopticon – a system of surveillance that encourages observers to internalise the gaze – so that families control their own children's behaviours in accordance with such ordinances so that the police rarely have to enforce them, in effect creating self-disciplining families. However, there is little consistent evidence that curfews have any impact on juvenile crime rates or social disorder (Matthew et al. 1999a). While the introduction of curfews in Houston and New Orleans (Campbell 1993, Morial 1995) produced some evidence of a drop in juvenile crime rates, other cities such as Baltimore have seen a rise in crime since the introduction of curfews (Bannerjee 1994), while in San Francisco the removal of a curfew was marked not, by the expected rise in arrests, but rather a drop of 16 per cent (Schiraldi 1996).

Justifying the introduction of a juvenile curfew in New Orleans, US, the Mayor claimed in a radio interview that 'It keeps teenagers off the streets. They need it, there's too many teenagers hanging around the streets'. It is not a view shared by the American Civil Liberties Union (ACLU). Curfews criminalise innocuous activities like walking on the street (Trollinger 1996), conceal the fact that some young people are on the streets to avoid violent and abusive situations at home or because they are financially excluded from commodified indoor recreational spaces (Matthews, Limb and Taylor 1999); and can increase hostility towards young people (Hodgkin 1998). The ACLU condemned the measure for targeting a powerless group of people who do not vote in order to enable politicians to claim that they are doing something about crime. It challenged the legality of curfews but lost when the US Supreme Court ruled that the first amendment does not give teenagers a generalised right of association that permits them to be out after hours and that official discrimination on the basis of age is possible.

Davis (1990) suggests that in Southern California residential curfews are deployed selectively against Black and Chicano youth. He writes: 'As a result of the war on drugs every non-Anglo teenager ... is now a prisoner of gang paranoia and associated demonology. Vast stretches of the region's sumptuous playgrounds, beaches and entertainment centers have become virtual no-go areas for young Blacks or Chicanos' (Davis 1990: 284). He cites several examples to make his point. In the first of which an off-duty black police officer, Don Jackson, took some 'ghetto kids' into an exclusive white area. Here, despite carefully obeying the law, the group were stopped and frisked, and Jackson was arrested for disturbing the peace. In the second example, a group of well-dressed Black members of Youth for Christ were on a visit to the Magic Mountains amusement park when, with no justification they were surrounded by security guards and searched for 'drugs and weapons'.

Whereas in the US this moral panic about young people is focused on gangs and is explicitly racialised, in the UK there has been a more general anxiety about what a British television documentary dubbed 'the end of childhood'.[2] It began in the mid 1990s with the murder of a two year-old, Jamie Bulger, by two ten year-old boys (Franklin and Petley 1996). Although, extremely unusual, this murder was not completely unprecedented and quickly became a reference point for other cases of violence committed by children. Other evidence, from statistics on bullying, joy-riding and teenage crime have been mobilised by the media to fuel popular anxieties about the unruliness of young people (Valentine 1996b, Jeffs and Smith 1996). Commenting on this phenomenon newspaper columnists and writers have made claims such as:

> The child has never been seen as such a menacing enemy as today. Never before have children been saturated with all the power of projected monstrousness to excite repulsion and even terror (Warner 1994: 43).

There is a growing uncertainty about the parameters of childhood and a mounting terror of the anarchy and uncontrollability of unfettered youth (Pilkington 1994: 18).

The demonisation of children has provided a new enemy within (Goldson 1997: 134).

While children have been labelled as the problem in this UK moral panic, the blame for their behaviour has been laid at the door of parents, schooling and the State. All three stand accused of having made children ungovernable by eroding the hierarchical relationship between adults and children. It is argued that parents have traditionally had 'natural' authority over their offspring as a result of their superior size, strength, age and command of material resources. An authority which has traditionally been sustained by the law and religion but also by everyday 'norms' about the appropriate behaviour of adults and children (Jamieson and Toynbee 1989). However, at end of the twentieth and beginning of the twenty-first centuries understandings about what it means to be a parent are alleged to have changed with adults voluntarily giving up some of their 'natural' authority in favour of closer and more equal relationships with their offspring (Ambert 1994, Wyness 1997). Harris (1983) for example, has argued that 'traditional' parental authority meant that parent-child conflicts were minimised because children had a moral obligation or duty to behave in certain ways towards their parents. Now, he claims the balance of obligations has shifted so that the responsibility is no longer on the child to be a dutiful son or daughter but on the parent to provide for their children in particular (mainly material) ways (see also Chapter Two). Indeed, in an individualised culture the stress is on children to be socialised into independence. As such Wyness (1997) suggests that parent/child relationships are problematic because parental ideas of setting boundaries as moral codes or guidelines can conflict with young people's demands for more autonomy.

This social change has also been accompanied by a general shift in both legal and popular attitudes to young people, away from an adults-know-best approach towards an emphasis on the personhood of the child and children's rights. As a result of which some commentators argue that there has been a decay in childhood as a separate category and that the distinction between children and adults is increasingly becoming blurred (Seabrook 1987). The growth in lone parent households has also meant that an increasing number of children are living in situations where they share emotional and financial responsibilities with a parent.

The extent to which parents have moved away from 'traditional authority' is Jamieson and Toynebee (1989) claim exemplified by changed attitudes to 'cheek'. They argue that 'whereas any kind of "talking back" or questioning of parental authority was considered a heinous crime in former times, parents nowadays appear to invite "discussion", viewing the talking-over of any problems as part of caring and sharing in family life' (Jamieson and Toynebee 1989: 97). On the basis of their research they further claim that this closeness has made parents in contemporary Western industrialised societies more vulnerable to children demands and less able or willing to control their children's behaviour than those of previous generations (Jamieson and Toynebee 1989), whilst Ambert (1994: 536) is more forthright stating that '[d]aily life offers evidence to the effect that adolescents have become less tolerant of parental supervision'.

As a result a number of studies have concluded that parents feel that they no longer have any moral or psychological resources to exercise authority over young people (Harris 1983, Wyness 1997). This mother and police officer describe their fears about the ungovernablity of contemporary young people:

Mother: I just think there's a whole different, you know, they're a lot less frightened of authority than we were, we'd have never done certain things that they do now I'm sure of that ... I don't think that they do have much respect for authority or older people now at all ... But like I say when ... they're all hanging around I find it really intimidating and to be, to feel like that about kids really, it's not nice to think that, not nice ('middle class' non-metropolitan area, Cheshire).

Police Officer: I've been in the Police 12 years and I've certainly found a difference in their [teenagers] attitude to the police and to people. I mean I can I know it sounds a bit corny or whatever but I remember when I was a lad I would never dream of shouting at some person walking down the street. But now they don't bother and that they do all sorts (Cheshire).

As these quotes suggest many parents hark back to the 'golden age' of their own childhood when children had respect for adults. Underlying this construction of 'respect' is an sometimes implicit, sometimes explicit, reference to regulatory regimes of discipline and violence that adults (parents, those acting *in loco parentis*, such as teachers, and the State) used (allegedly) in public and in private as a deterrent and as a punishment to keep children under control. Now, parents argue that children's rights campaigners, such as EPOCH (End Physical Punishment of Children) have undermined the foundations on which this respect was built. Firstly, because they have encouraged a shift in both legal and popular attitudes to children, away from an 'adults know best' approach, towards an emphasis on the personhood of children (for example, if it is wrong to hit a person it must also be wrong to hit a child). Secondly, and perhaps most significantly in the eyes of the parents, teachers and police interviewed, the State has increasingly adopted a liberal line towards the physical punishment of children (for example, child minders are not permitted to smack children, and State schools are no longer able to use corporal punishment to discipline pupils) and has therefore removed the ultimate tool adults (parents, those who act *in loco parentis*, such as teachers, and the police) had at their disposal to enforce their authority and superiority in both private and public space. These perceptions have been further accentuated by changes in contemporary policing which have resulted in forces becoming organisationally and operationally divorced from the public, and a perceived decline in neighbourhood community (Herbert 1998). These adults explain:

> Mother: I think if we had more powers, like if I could go up to somebody and give them a clip round the earhole without me facing an assault charge, then yes, we could stop it. But we can't stop it anymore they're [kids] have got a free rein ... nothing anybody can do about it. If they get arrested it's just practically, you know. 'Don't do it again, naughty boy and off you go ('middle class', non-metropolitan town, Cheshire).

> Father: They don't discipline them anymore. You know, they're [schools and police] not allowed to touch them anymore, so they can get away with a lot more. There's no corporal punishment and I think that's wrong. They're making their own decisions in life, that's what it is – The parents are not making the decisions for children. We were brought up to respect the elders – honestly, I mean I sound old fashioned but that is the way we were brought up at school. Like now they just do what they want to do and like no-one can change what they do ('middle class', metropolitan area, Greater Manchester).

> Mother: I think it's getting to the stage where you can't control children. You know you daren't smack 'em, you daren't reprimand them in front of somebody else, otherwise they've only got to utter a word in school and you've got the Social Services knocking on the door ... So I think that's why children are like they are, because the schools can't give 'em the cane anymore; you daren't smack 'em anymore, so they know that they're going to be able to get away with it, so they just do it because they know there's nothing you can do to stop it ('working class', metropolitan area, Greater Manchester).

> Father: I know if I ever got into trouble, I mean you hear it in the papers now a copper's clipped a lad's ear and he's in court. I know when I were a lad, if a copper clipped my ear and I'd told me mother she'd have given me another one you know, it's all sort of changed now ('working class', rural area, Derbyshire).

This moral panic about both child violence and the ungovernability of children is being used to justify adults' perceptions that contemporary young people – particularly teenagers – are a threat to their hegemony on the street. As a result this moral panic is being used to mobilise a consensus which (as in the US) is being used to justify various strategies to restrict young people's access to, and freedoms in, 'public' space (Valentine 1996a, 1996b). The 1998 *Crime and Disorder Act* established procedures for local authorities to introduce street curfews for children under 10. In 2003 this scheme was extended to cover children up to the age of 16. The police can now apply for curfew orders, lasting from 9pm to 6am, which would cover a known 'trouble spot', such as a town centre or part of a housing estate for a period of 90 days. However, these measures have not yet extended as far as the more expansive

US style curfews described above. Indeed, in the first five years of the curfew scheme for children under 10 no local authorities actually applied for the designated powers to keep children off the street. Rather, a range of piecemeal restrictions are being imposed on young people's use of space. These include: the use of closed circuit television to track and exclude young people from spaces such as shopping malls (Fyfe and Bannister 1998); bye-laws to prevent young people playing football in streets (Wyn and White 1997) and on grassed areas; truancy watch schemes to encourage the public policing of young people in everyday spaces (James and Jenks 1996); and the introduction of new powers for the police and local authorities enabling them to impose fines on young people for anti-social or nuisance behaviour (Travis 2003). These sorts of practice have been dubbed by Wyn and White (1997) as a form of spatial apartheid.

As a result, young people are increasingly regarded as a polluting presence on the streets. The police control the street in three ways. First, the physical presence of uniforms on the street provides symbolic reassurance of order and control. Second, the police use active surveillance to monitor behaviour of those in public. Third, they intervene to establish order. Most of this 'peace keeping' is done without invoking the power of the law through arrest but through 'rough informality' such as controlling people's behaviour in space or moving people or groups between spaces (although, this form of policing relies on individuals and groups complying with officers' requests). As the police officer explains below controlling young people's behaviour on the street takes up an important part of officers' time, usually involving a geographical game of cat and mouse, in which the police push them from one space to another, yet in most cases the teenagers are not committing any offence (a similar pattern of community surveillance, complaints and neighbourhood policing is described by Baumgartner, 1988, in a study of a suburb on the eastern seaboard of the US). Such tactics represent what Sibley (1988) has termed in another context, 'the purification of space' which he defines as 'the rejection of difference and the securing of boundaries to maintain homogeneity'. Through using the police in this way, residents attempt to maintain the moral order of the suburbs. This police officer describes his role in restricting young people's use of public space:

Police Officer: I worked there for 4 years in a police car ... Your busy shift would be the afternoon shift till late in the evening. And you would on a busy day perhaps get 20 plus incidents. And maybe 7 or maybe more dealing with what we call Youth Causing Annoyance. And it would sometimes be young people gathering together and it might be an old lady disturbed by the noise they're making. And she makes a phone call can you come down and move them on. We go down and do that but when we've gone they come back again. Or maybe its running across gardens and setting hedges on fire, general vandalism. I would think if we didn't have that problem our job would be a lot easier. Its incessant. It goes on and on (Greater Manchester).

To justify such adult spatial hegemony either, Qvortrup (1994) has argued albeit in a different context, that adults must always be read as qualitatively more important than children/teenagers or they must always act in accordance with the best interest of children. If, as Qvortrup (1994) argues, neither of these arguments holds water then we must question why the production and management of public space requires children and teenagers to be treated as human becomings, not human beings.

The Death of Truly 'Public' Space?

As Chapter One argued public space is not just 'there' but is something that is actively produced through repeated performances. The previous chapters have shown how repetitive performances of young children as vulnerable and incompetent (including media reports of abductions, 'stranger-danger' style education campaigns and parental controls on children's spatial activities) are congealing to facilitate the production of public space as an adult space where unaccompanied youngsters do not belong. While older children are credited with the competence to negotiate public space safely, this chapter has argued that nevertheless teenagers are expected to show deference to adults, and adults' definitions of appropriate behaviour, levels of noise and so on. Thus again, exposing the extent of the underlying adult assumption that public space is not a space shared on an equal footing by all generations, but rather is a space that is taken for granted as the realm of grown-ups.

Further this chapter has shown that the regulatory framework (largely forms of physical discipline, such as corporal punishment) that has been, up until recently, attributed with maintaining adult hegemony in public space has been unpicked, leading to a panic (that has echoes through history) that 'natural' adult authority is being eroded. This panic is being used to win popular support for a range of strategies to regulate and restrict young people's use of space. Such collisions between adults and young people over the use of space have resulted in a decline in the availability of places where teenagers can develop independent identities as they make transition to adulthood (Aitken 2001). The hostility and aggressiveness of adults towards young people's exertion of difference on the streets is therefore becoming an index of adult power.

Public space has traditionally been understood as a popular space which we all have access to, where we meet strangers (Sennett 1993), and thus encounter 'difference' (Young 1990). Above all, public space has been defined as a space of unmediated interactions where people can just go and 'be' (Mitchell 1996). Zukin (1995: 262) summarises 'the defining characteristics of urban public space [as] proximity, diversity and accessibility', claiming that '[t]he questions of who can occupy public space, and so define an image of the city, is open-ended' (Zukin 1995: 11). As such, public spaces like the street are often romanticised and celebrated as a site of authentic political action, as a place of inclusiveness and therefore as inherently democratic spaces (Sorkin 1992). However, the efforts of the adults to restrict young people's freedom on the street, that have been described in this chapter, call into question to what extent these places can truly be called 'public' if their maintenance requires the marginalisation or exclusion of teenagers and young people. First urban renewal schemes, state planners and corporate enterprises are combining to produce carefully monitored and controlled privatised 'public' environments 'that are based on desires for security rather than interaction' (Mitchell 1995: 119), and from which young people are largely excluded. Second, legal (e.g. curfews, bye-laws etc.) and policing initiatives, largely driven by adults fear, are being used to filter young people out of public spaces in order to reproduce an adultist moral order on the streets.

Through such measures 'public' space is being drained of its vitality and meaning. Free expression is being prohibited and the democratic mix of the street is being undermined. This in turn is putting young people's, and other so-called undesirable groups' (e.g. the homeless, those with mental ill-health and so on) legitimacy as members of the public in doubt (Mitchell 1995). Some pessimists (Sorkin 1992, Sennett 1993) have gone so far as to proclaim that such measures mark death of the street and the end of truly public space. For these writers the maintenance of 'public' space requires its frequent use by a wide mixture of people. Berman (1986) for example, is opposed to the privatisation and commodification of 'public' space. He argues that space fails not when it is full of so-called 'deviants' but when they are absent. He writes:

> there isn't much point in having public space, unless problematical people are free to come into the centre of the scene ... The glory of modern public space is that it can pull together all the different sorts of people who are there. It can both compel and empower these people to see each other, not through a glass darkly but face to face (Berman 1986: 482).

This is an argument for open-minded space: space that is open to encounters between people of different ages, classes, races, religions, ideologies, cultures and stances towards life. Thus the central issue for Berman is to find ways of resolving these differences that preserve 'public' space by sustaining its shared use, rather than diminishing and destroying it by exclusion. He states that 'No doubt there would be all sorts of dissonance and conflict and trouble in this [open minded] space' – but he argues – 'that would be exactly what we'd be after. In a genuinely open space, all of a city's loose ends can hang out, all of a society's inner contradictions can express and unfold themselves' (Berman 1986: 484). It is a view also evident in the work of Sennett. He claims that 'The public realm should be gritty and disturbing rather than pleasant' and that disorder and painful events are important 'because they force us to engage with "otherness", to go beyond one's own defined boundaries of self, and are thus central to civilised and civilising social life' (Sennett 1996: 131–2). To this end there is a need for public space to be planned to attract all different populations, across the generations, and to be discreetly policed. The final chapter addresses these issues by considering the question of children and young people's citizenship and how to involve them in participatory and planning frameworks.

Notes

1   Privacy embraces: ability to control space, ability to be alone or free from disturbance and the ability to manage the performance of and information about the self in the past and present (Wolfe 1978).
2   While these US and UK moral panics both appear to be a contemporary phenomena, it is worth noting that adults fears of, and hostility towards the younger generation have been extremely widespread over the centuries. Pearson (1983) observes that there have been complaints about young people's moral degeneracy and criminality for over 150 years. He cites examples of scares about 'cosh boys' and 'Blitz kids' during the Second World War as well as a string of moral panics about young people's misuse of leisure time in the inter war years.

Chapter 7

Children and the Future of Public Space

Children are at the heart of contemporary debates about public space. On the one hand the late twentieth and early twenty-first centuries have witnessed increased popular concern in North America and Europe about young children's vulnerability to sexual assault and murder in public space. This anxiety about children's safety appears to be profoundly affecting relationships between adults and children in public places. On the other hand, there appears to be a simultaneous rising tide of adult fear about the anarchy and uncontrollability of young people. Moral panics about everything from child murderers, and teenage gangs, to juvenile crime rates are being elided to fuel adults' fears that public space is being overrun by dangerous adolescents, threatening others' personal safety and disrupting the moral order of the street.

This book has traced these twin concerns. Chapter One began by highlighting the historical origins and continuity of these juxtaposed understandings of children as both vulnerable 'angels' in need of protection from the adult world and unruly, menacing 'devils' in need of discipline and containment. The following chapters explored these conceptualisations of young people in the context of the contemporary moral landscape of childhood.

Chapter Two outlined the extent of contemporary fears about young children's safety in relation to actual patterns of harm. It showed that there is a geography to parents' fears. Mothers and fathers regard their children to be most at risk from strangers in public space, despite the fact that statistically children are more at risk in private space from people known to them. There is also a popular belief that contemporary children are more vulnerable to danger in public space than today's adults were during their own childhoods, although there is no evidence to support this perception. Indeed, while most parents recognise that the risk of their own child being murdered is slight, within the context of the contemporary 'risk society', they are also aware that risk assessment and decision making is an increasingly important feature of daily life. Children are highly valued in contemporary society in both personal and emotional (rather than economic) terms. Parents are responsible for them achieving or fulfilling their opportunities and promise, and therefore for their risk management. As such parents' own personal identities are increasingly understood in terms of their child-rearing practices, which means that their responses to their children's safety are framed in terms of their own self images as parents. Moreover parents are aware that if anything were to happen to their child, not only would they feel responsible and blame themselves but others would blame them too. Most therefore choose to restrict their children's outdoor play because the consequences of not doing so and losing a child make the risk not worthwhile. Parents' everyday risk management is informed by a range of sources of information, including the media, and vicarious and personal experience, all of which are interpreted and made sense of within the context of local communities producing subtly different geographies of fear.

The chapter concluded by looking at the way adults try to develop children's skills to manage and take risks for themselves. It concluded that this personal safety education paints a misleading picture of stranger-danger in public space versus the safety of the home and demonises unknown men. As such children are encouraged to withdraw from public space and to avoid interactions with strangers, which contributes towards producing public space as an adult space where they are not able to participate freely. This has further consequences in that children are not made aware of the possibility that the family home might also be a site of abuse; and the exaggeration of the public danger message can also serve as a means of protecting the adult world from the intrusion of children.

Parental cultures of protectionism were the focus of Chapter Three. It began by highlighting how fears for children's safety have evolved from being primarily framed in terms of girls' vulnerability, to include boys too. It then went onto argue that it is impossible to separate out parental risk assessment from the construction of what it means to be a 'good' parent. The chapter outlined the production of local geographies of parenting and considered gender differences in terms of mothers' and fathers' roles in managing children's use of space. While parental attitudes to the gendered nature of risk appear to be changing, the chapter showed that parenting is still conducted largely on traditional gender lines. Although the culture of fatherhood and the conduct of motherhood have both shifted significantly in recent decades, mothers still bear the burden of caring for and supervising their children on a daily basis, while fathers in most households adopt the role of disciplinarian. The importance of place, class and ethnic identities were also evident in the construction of 'local norms' about what it means to be a 'good' mother. The chapter concluded by drawing attention to the way that gender divisions of childcare responsibilities can be more complicated in reconstituted families where parenting is shared between 'biological' mothers and fathers who live apart, and 'social' fathers.

In Chapter Four the focus switched to how parents' general understandings of children's competence to negotiate public space safely, and their ideals about children's spatial boundaries, are translated into practice in the context of the realities of everyday domestic life. This chapter showed that children are active social agents in their own lives who negotiate and contest understandings of their 'competence' and spatial freedoms with their parents. Here competence was understood not as a fixed measure associated with biological age but rather as a performative concept that is established through repetition within a regulatory framework that includes the media and local parenting cultures. The emphasis was also on the ability of children to resist and subvert rules laid down by parents. At the same time it also demonstrated that when children do encounter dangerous situations they can be mature and rational about the ways that they handle them. Children describe their parents' fears in irrational, over emotional, less reasoned terms; terms that are usually defined as the characteristics of childhood. In this sense, children can be more like adults and vice versa such that competence needs not to be thought of as a stable attribute of a particular age but rather as a fluid context-dependent performance that can be staged by children and adults alike.

The consequence of parents' protectionist cultures for young children's use of space was the focus of Chapter Five. This chapter showed that parental fears, (exacerbated by the erosion of public space for children caused by disinvestment) have led to a retreat from the street. Outdoor play is now more home-centred and children are now spending increasing amounts of leisure time engaged in institutionalised (and often education or skills development) activities rather than independent free play. The commodification of children's safety in the form of these specialist places for children has effectively led to the corralling of young people, while the elision of these spaces with notions of public space has obscured the extent to which the public realm is being privatised. As a result, children's play is increasingly structured by adults, robbing children of the opportunities to develop spatial knowledge and skills, self reliance, their own street cultures, experiment with their identities, and enjoy rich and imaginative play experiences. The trade-off being that instead young people are being offered the opportunity to develop their potential in terms of new skills (music, sport etc.) and knowledge, along with the added cultural and social capital that goes with such experiences. The chapter concluded by highlighting the unequal opportunities that children of different socio-economic backgrounds have to experience institutionalised leisure and free play and considered some of the consequences of these differences. Namely, while more heavily chaperoned 'middle class' children are usually perceived to have the better (i.e. more privatised/institutionalised) play opportunities, it is the children from lone parent households whose play is more independent and 'public' focused, and who therefore may well have the richest environmental experiences.

In Chapter Six, the focus switched from the vulnerability of young children in public space to the disruption and disorder that teenagers are perceived to bring to public space. It argued that as a result of age discrimination in public venues, the commodification of malls/leisure centres and disinvestments in public spaces like youth clubs, teenagers have nowhere to go and so hang around on the streets. Space – even when shared by adults and children – is used in different ways for different purposes, causing inevitable collisions in use and values. Young people's behaviour is not read as part of the vitality of the streets but rather as potentially threatening and dangerous, and disruptive of the moral order of the street.

At the same time the regulatory framework (largely forms of physical discipline, such as corporal punishment) that has been, up until recently, attributed with maintaining adult hegemony in public space, has according to the media, politicians, parents and police been unpicked, leading to a moral panic that 'natural' adult authority is being eroded. This panic is being used to win popular support a range of strategies to regulate young people's use of space. By advocating such measures, the media and politicians, and the police and parents interviewed in this project, implicitly assume that public space belongs to adults. The hostility and aggressiveness of adults towards young people's exertion of difference articulates adult insecurities about their ability to maintain this production of space. Furthermore, this othering of young people has also been identified as part of a much wider process of the commodification and privatisation of 'public' space.

In summary therefore, this book has argued that understandings of young children as at risk of crime; and older children as a threat to the moral order of public space, both lead to public space being produced as an adult space where children do not properly belong. To this extent it is questionable whether public space can truly be regarded as 'public'. Yet, as Chapter One outlined, there is nothing inherent about the nature of public space. It is not merely a backdrop for social relations, a pre-existing terrain which frames everyday life. Rather public space is the product of relations and as such space is always in the process of becoming, taking on new forms as different interests are continually interacting and struggling for influence, and so can always be remade. In other words, there is no need to accept adultist space as the natural order rather it is important to think about what needs to be done to produce socio-spatial relations differently.

First, we need to protect what Aitken (2001: 176) has termed children's 'thick' play (see Chapter Five) which he defined as 'the active exploration of individual and social imaginaries, built up in the spaces of everyday life'. This means challenging the commodification and privatisation of both children/ childhood, and public space that are leading to the corralling of children in institutional spaces and the loss of truly open public space. This needs to be achieved by challenging cultures of disinvestment in the public sphere to create safe public open space (rather than privatised so-called 'public' spaces) in local communities where young people have the privacy to play or be free from the panopticon gaze and control of adults, yet still within a framework of guidance and protection. In doing so, such a strategy might serve to revitalise local 'communities' and unpick local parenting cultures predicated on excessive fear and risk management.

Second, we need to challenge the demonisation of teenagers by providing them with public places that meet their needs, and from which they are not marginalised as a result of age discrimination, financially excluded as a result of the commodification of leisure/retail and entertainment spaces, or denied because of disinvestment in public facilities, such as community centres and youth clubs. This would involve a recognition that some of teenagers' troublesome activities like graffiti and vandalism, are usually not motivated by malicious intent but rather are a product of the disconnection and disaffection that young people feel because of the way that they are excluded from 'adult' environments in part at least, because of the way that the physical environment has been designed and managed with a lack of understanding of young people's needs or provision of resources or space for them. The danger is that if we fail to provide public spaces that meet young people's needs while at the same time policing and limiting their use of neighbourhood streets (especially at night) young people may be driven into more marginal spaces and consequently be placed in more danger.

Both of these strategies mean moving away from an emphasis on children as a problem that either need to be corralled for their own safety, or contained for other people's safety. Rather then, we need to focus on children's rights to use public space safely, and on producing spaces that meet the needs of both young children and teenagers/young people. This means challenging sensational and irresponsible media coverage of both stranger-dangers and troublesome teens, acknowledging that young people have views on public space, and addressing what young people need to become involved in appropriate participatory and planning frameworks (Hart 1992). At the same time it is important not to universalise what it means to be a child or a young person. Although, socio-spatial marginalisation is a feature of western child-hoods, as most of the chapters in this book have demonstrated, some children experience it more than, or in different ways from others. It is therefore important to understand children and young people's diverse experiences of their childhoods and public space.

The Right to Participate: Children and Citizenship

Citizenship refers to the relationships between individuals and the community or state within which they live (Smith 1989). The expectation is that members of a state have duties and obligations/responsibilities towards it but that in return they can expect certain rights and benefits (Marshall 1950). These include *civil* or *legal rights* (freedom of speech, assembly, movement, equality before the law); *political rights* (to vote, engage in political activity, hold office etc.) and *social rights* (to welfare, a basic standard of living etc.). Despite the fact that the language of citizenship is framed round inclusion and universality it is also an exclusionary practice (Lister 1997). Historically, only select groups – notably white property owning men – have been entitled to full citizenship. Other groups (such as women and ethnic, cultural and religious minority groups) have had to fight for the gradual extension of their rights. Children still largely lie outside of this framework, being excluded from, or at best only having limited forms of, civil, legal, political and social rights.

According to Matthews and Limb (1998) since the nineteenth century the legislative system of the western world has contributed to the exclusion of children from planning and consequently having a say in the shaping of their own environments. A recent survey of architects, planners and designers found that most rarely considered the specific needs of children, and that they had little knowledge about how children use public space in practice (White 2001). Yet, children's interests, values and spatial practices are not necessarily the same as those of adults (Kelley et al. 1997). In so far as children or other marginalised groups remain invisible in public space in this way, they fail to be counted as legitimate members of the polity. And in this sense, public spaces are essential to the functioning of democratic politics.

Unlike other marginalized social groups, children are relatively powerless to articulate their own views and environmental needs, and to challenge adultist practices and processes through public forums such as the media and the law. While those aged 16 and over have more opportunities and resources to represent their own views through the media, and to participate, at least to some extent, in the democratic process (even though they may not be able to vote until 18), several studies have demonstrated that at a national level there is widespread disinterest and apathy on the part of young people towards politics. O'Toole (2003), for example, suggests that young people feel excluded from, or marginalized within, mainstream politics because of their youth; they feel that issues specific to young people are not included on agendas; and that there is a lack of resources and community facilities provided for them. As such, young people appear to be opting out of participation in conventional party politics (Barnardos 1996, Furlong and Cartmel 1997), although there is evidence of their growing involvement in local or single issue campaign groups where they often have a stronger voice and more opportunities to participate fully (Eden and Roker 2000, Hodgkin and Newell 1996).

The Children's Rights Office has estimated that children in the UK aged under 18 represent a disenfranchised group of 13 million (Matthews and Limb 1998). It is an absence from representation that has been dubbed the democratic deficit (Lansdown 1995).

Children are excluded from full citizenship because of modern conceptions of childhood (outlined in Chapter One) that regard children as vulnerable and dependent on adults. The implication being that young people are incomplete or passive actors, adults in-waiting, who do not have the competence or autonomy to participate in society in their own right (despite the fact that in previous centuries young people engaged in paid work, and were involved in the social, sexual and political landscape at a much earlier age). Yet, as Chapters Four and Six have illustrated, children are active agents in their own lives, who can make sense of their own worlds and shape their own environments (see also Alanen 1990, Prout and James 1990, Waksler 1986).

Other adult misconceptions that have precluded children's participation include firstly, a belief amongst some adults that extending children's rights would threaten adults' natural authority to decide what is best for young people. However, this presupposes that adults both know what young people need/want and then act in a way that supports children's best interests, when in practice this is not always the case (Qvortrup et al. 1994). Secondly, some adults believe that children should not have rights until they can exercise responsibilities. Yet children are regarded as having criminal responsibilities at the age of 10 and sexual responsibility at the age of 16 (Matthew et al. 1999). Moreover, in practice, few children live an idealised existence free from any responsibilities, and some bear very heavy burdens, for example, acting as carers for sick relatives or interpreters for parents (Stables and Smith 1999). Finally, some adults argue that giving children responsibilities would undermine their right to a childhood that is free from the concerns of adulthood. This ignores the fact that young people's lives are, in any event, full of everyday worries (for example, about examinations, friendships and family relationships, bullying, body shape and size and so on) (Lansdown 1995).

Because children do not have a framework or opportunity to participate as full citizens there has been increasing recognition of the need to create a space for their voices to be heard. The case for young people's representation has been taken up on the international stage (Rosenbaum and Newell 1991). In 1989, the UN Convention on the Rights of the Child (UNCRC) established the right of children to participate in society. Specifically, Article 12 affirms children's rights to express their views and to have those views heard, Article 13 provides for their rights to freedom of expression, Article 14 addresses freedom of thought, Article 15 deals with the right to association and assembly, and Article 29 covers the right to an education that will encourage responsible citizenship. Effectively, the UNCRC provides a vision of a dialogue between young people and government at all levels from local to global (Freeman 1996).

The UNCRC is important because it potentially opens up fundamental changes to our culture. The intention is not to give children equal rights to make decisions with their care-givers, neither is it to disrupt the authority of parents, nor to extend to children all the rights afforded to adults (Archard 1993). Rather, the UNCRC recognises that children still depend on the caring decisions of adults, but that adults need to have an openness to listen to and communicate with children (Hart 1997).

Implicitly, this embraces a recognition that children's rights should relate to their capacity rather than to their biological age. As Chapter Four highlighted, Piagetian (1952) models of age related stages of development assume a qualitative difference between the ability of children and adults that closes as young people progress along a linear continuum of growth. This develop-mental understanding of competence – that biological age determines ability – has now been overtaken by a contextual or relational conceptualisation of children's competence. This recognises that competence is predicated on factors such as a child's understanding of relevant information and issues, their wisdom or ability to make choices in their own best interests, and their freedom to do so without coercion (Alderson 1995, Morrow and Richards

1996, Valentine 1999c). This also potentially allows for some recognition of, and sensitivity towards, children's different emotional and intellectual skills and competences, rather than universalising or homogenising young people.

The UNCRC potentially has wide ranging implications across all spheres of life. Hart (1997) in particular, advocates children's right to appeal against adult decisions and for the need for adults to justify the wisdom of their decisions rather than just stating 'it is the law', or 'that's how it is'. He also calls for a more radical social science in which children themselves can learn to reflect upon their own conditions, so that they can gradually begin to take greater responsibility in creating communities different from the ones that they inherit (Hart 1997). To such ends he puts forward a typology of adult-child engagement, that ranges from manipulation and tokenism to child-initiated shared decisions with adults. Aitken (2001) suggest that this vision has echoes of Bunge's (1977) aim to revolutionise adult/child power relations to promote children as the 'privileged class'.

The United Nations has set up a Committee on the Rights of the Child to monitor the success of its convention. Its findings suggest that progress is patchy. The Council of Europe launched the European charter on the participation of young people in municipal and regional life in 1992. This advocated the need for local authorities and regions across Europe to implement policies to foster young people's participation in community life and for structures to be developed to enable young people's representation, consultation and co-management (Matthews et al. 1999). Across Europe there are a number of successful participatory organisations co-ordinated by national agencies that are working towards involving young people more effectively in local decision making about their communities. For example, Switzerland has a Association of Youth Parliaments funded by the Federal Cultural Office and the Swiss Association of Youth Organisations (Ludescher 1997); in Italy there is a National Association of Children's Councils (Castellani 1997); and in France the Association Nationale des Conseils d'Enfants et de Jeunes is responsible for a network of children and youth town councils across the country (Jodry 1997). Norway has perhaps been the country to respond most seriously to the UNCRC by appointing a children's ombudsman (Flekkoy 1995).

In the UK the development of youth councils and forums has been piecemeal and *ad hoc*. While there are now over 200 different youth councils across the country they are scattered unevenly across England, Scotland, Wales and Northern Ireland (Matthews et al. 1999b). This reflects the fact that with no national legislation or guidelines in place to promote children's participation and rights, the existence of youth councils and forums, and the extent to which they are successful depends on the political make up and traditions of particular localities; the efforts and charisma of individuals; and the nature of existing institutional structures. Moreover, unlike the situation in France where there is there is a single organisation responsible for youth councils, there is little communication or coordination between them so that they do not learn from each others' experiences. All of which contributes to perceptions that they are risky and experimental. As a result of which, young people's forums are still outside the mainstream of planning (Matthews et al. 1999).

More generally however, local governments in the UK are increasingly aware of the need to encourage young people's participation in their activities and decision making because of the *Children's Act* of 1989. This covers a wide range of measures. It is most notable for marking a legal departure from children being regarded as passive recipients of adult decisions towards becoming legal subjects in their own right. It instructs the courts to have particular regard to children's feelings and wishes and gives them the right to have information on decisions affecting them. As such there are increasingly more attempts by local governments to work with young people, both to show that they are consulting this community and because of the need to be seen tackling the 'youth problem' outlined in Chapter Six (Wynn and White 1997). Politically, such consultation exercises also have the advantage of increasing young people's political awareness and skills, and potentially of winning future voters.

However, such initiatives tend to have limited effectiveness. The hierarchical power structure of local government mitigates against young people's participation or ability to get their voice heard; resources/budgets are not specifically allocated for young people's participation; and local government is driven by election and bureaucratic time frames which may not facilitate the participation of young people. The participation agenda is often foisted onto professionals (such as planners, architects, social workers, community workers, youth workers, councillors and so on) rather than being initiated by these groups themselves (Freeman et al. 2003). As such some professionals consult young people because they are obliged to, rather than because they are committed to this process. They often have little training or experience of working with youth professionals let alone young people themselves. This means that where participation is carried out professionals often unwittingly adopt adultist formats that involve children attending committees and public meetings, or setting up youth forums that are ultimately controlled and structured by adults (Freeman et al. 2003). Because these forms of participation effectively absorb young people into adultist institutional structures, rather than treating children and adults as equal partners, they are usually not very empowering for young people and represent only tokenism (Storrie 1997). Not surprisingly professionals can find it hard to recruit young people to participate in these sorts of consultation and are sceptical about their effectiveness because young people are often bored and confused by their role (Jamison and Gilbert 2000, Hart and Schwab 1997).

Professionals also have a tendency only to consult young people on issues such as recreation and entertainment – that are perceived by adults to be young people's issues – rather than broader issues that can equally impact on their everyday lives. Likewise, there is a danger of universalising childhood on the basis of consultation exercises carried out with particular types of young people, namely the more educated, articulate middle classes. Instead of which there is a need to think and speak of childhoods and adults in the plural, and to accommodate a recognition of 'difference' in terms of children's identities and experiences within consultative frameworks.

Even where young people's views are sought in a positive way, the young people themselves are often cynical that nothing will change. Consultation exercises usually focus on children's past experiences and plans for the future, not on changing the now of the childhood that the young people are actually experiencing at the time (Caputo 1995). Because the time-scale of policy implementation can be very slow, and because children tend to be very focused on the present (Holloway and Valentine 2003), it can be difficult for them to recognise any positive outcomes that may arise from their involvement in participatory exercises.

This is not to say that consultation exercises are a waste of time. Rather there is a need to develop more effective ways of involving young people. In particular, to provide adults who can be skilled at facilitating young people's participation (Smith 2003) and to provide more positive outcomes from consultation. The notion of young people's rights and responsibilities and skills of citizenship need to be nurtured/developed from a very early age. Effective involvement of young people in local consultation and decision making throughout their childhoods would provide young people with an education in democracy rather than suddenly having democratic responsibility thrust on them with no preparation when they gain the vote at age 18 (Hart 1997, Satterthwaite et al. 1996). It might also give children the practical and social skills to start to play a part in community life (Adams and Ingham 1998) and, in particular, to develop a sense of empowerment and 'ownership' of the places and communities within which they live (Hungerford and Volk 1990).

Moreover, it is important not only to think of children's rights and partici-pation in a uni-directional sense – what children can gain – but rather also to recognise what adults/professionals and communities can learn from young people (Aitken 2001). For example, as Chapter Four illustrated, children's everyday lives are very strongly embedded in their local neighbourhood communities, and they therefore have much more understanding of, and investment in them, than most adults. The participation of children in local decision making can therefore be a catalyst for adults also to become more involved in communities and planning (Hart 1997). Recognising that their children have a place and a role in the local community may also encourage some parents to acknowledge their children's competencies and so begin to challenge overly protectionist local parenting cultures.

Communities are crucial in tackling fears for children's safety, and the demonisation of young people because they represent important ways through which people lives are woven into the public sphere. As Chapters

Two to Six have demonstrated, while fear of crime and the exclusion of teenagers are national, and to some extent even global, processes that are evident in all of the neighbourhoods in which this research was based (urban and rural, 'working class' and 'middle class'), they are also played out differently in different localities. This is apparent in terms of the ways that the media and vicarious information about dangers are interpreted (Chapter Two), local understandings of what it means to be a good parent (Chapter Three); the extent to which children engage in institutionalised activities and/ or independent environmental exploration (Chapter Five); and the extent to which, and where, teenagers hang out and are perceived to disrupt the street (Chapter Six). As such local socio-spatial relations need to be understood as products of interaction, neither entirely closed and local, nor universal and undifferentiated (Massey 1998, Holloway and Valentine 2000).

As Chapter Two demonstrated, strong neighbourhood communities can help mediate parental fears by providing natural surveillance through the presence of 'eyes on the street' (Jacobs 1961) and a sense of social cohesion and security. In many places, however, such close-knit social relations have declined as affluence and mobility mean that people no longer know or rely on each other in the same way as in the past. Planning with, and for children, offers one possible mechanism for kick-starting such neighbourly relations, and bringing both children and adults onto the street. In this way, the blossoming of such relations might also help to tackle the more general decay in public space and the rise in citizen fear outlined in Chapter Six.

Finally, as Chapter Three showed, local communities (especially emerging from activities such as collecting children from school or institutional activities, parent teachers associations etc.) provide an important arena for relaying information and negotiating shared parenting cultures, particularly in terms of moral rules about what it means to be a 'good' parent. These sites of communication, as mediating links between identities and practices, therefore provide an important intervention point to tackle parents' misplaced geographies of fear and excessive risk management. Notably, parental concerns about children's safety are often informed largely by sensational media reports about rare crimes against children at a national or international level. Given that such stories both sell newspapers and provide a good editing device (see Chapter Two) it is unlikely that the media will respond to any pressures to provide more balanced reporting of the threats posed to, and by, children and young people. At the same time parents frequently complain about the lack of information they receive about the risks in their specific localities.

It is through local communities (via schools and institutional activities for children) therefore that the police and local authorities might most effectively disseminate regular updates about local crime (or lack of it). The picture provided might then reassure parents that contemporary anxieties about stranger-dangers in public space are generally over exaggerated. It would also enable them to tailor their parenting practices, particularly the time-space restrictions they put on their children, according to actual local threats. Through such processes parents may begin to collectively renegotiate what it means to be a 'good parent' and local parenting cultures and to ignore the more sensationalist accounts of stranger-dangers and dangerous youth.

In other words, such strategies for tackling the crisis of childhood have some echoes of communitarianism in that they regard community as a resource that can be used to foster a more democratic society, and recognise that social problems can be addressed at very localised scales and are predicated on respect for children's rights (Etzioni 1993).

Given children's general lack of voice and the need for a more community oriented approach to the crisis of childhood, the concluding section of this chapter reflects on some of the ways local governments might address the question of children's citizenship and community.

Implementing Children's Citizenship

Bartlett et al. (1999) provide an outline of the practical implications for local governments if they are to accept their responsibilities to respond to the rights and requirements of children and young people. They argue that if local governments are to promote children's rights then institutions need to reflect the goals of the UNCRC in their frameworks, and establish local plans of action for young people (that should ideally link to a national plan) as part of an on-going process, not a one-off effort. All local regulations and action plans must be made to comply with these goals. Above all local governments need to demonstrate these priorities through the allocation of resources and their budgeting decisions.

In order to realise children's rights, local governments would also need to use participatory methods both in problem identification and in the collection and analysis of local data. This means involving children as partners, and developing participatory frameworks that are sensitive to the differences concerning the social categories of children and youth. An example of this in practice includes the UNESCO Management of Social Transformation Programme's international project, *Growing up in Cities*, that is involving children and young people from eight countries in assessing their urban environment and planning how to change them (Chawla 2002).

Children's issues extend across all areas of local government from housing and education to health and juvenile justice. As such, planning for the protection of children requires a recognition on behalf of authorities of the integration of children's needs in different spheres and therefore the importance of co-ordinating different services. Bartlett et al. (1999) suggest that this might best be achieved by establishing a body to oversee the actions of local government, its effects on children and its adherence to children's rights. Perhaps, for example, creating a separate agency for children's affairs that can oversee information-sharing, joint-planning etc. Measures would also be needed to extend these principles into local practice. Here, community development liaison officers might provide a link between neighbourhoods and government agencies, and help to draw in the most marginalized and excluded groups. Codes of conduct for professional practice also need to be established that reflect the obligations of professionals to understand and respond to children and young people's rights and requirements. Finally, a mechanism for enforcement needs to be put in to place to ensure that all of these goals are realised.

This acceptance and implementation of children's citizenship would mean a cultural change. As such local governments would also have an important role to play in providing information and education about the UNCRC because unless people are accurately informed they will lack an understanding of the process and the basis for participation. In doing so, they would also need to promote a participatory culture within communities, and establish ways for the effective representation of the most vulnerable and excluded members of communities. An essential part of this process would be the provision of information to all stakeholders in an accessible form (for example, in different language formats or different media, like videos and cartoons).

By claiming space in public, and becoming more centrally involved in the creation of public spaces, children and young people themselves become public, and can begin to be counted as legitimate members of the polity. In this way, by truly opening a door to groups as disenfranchised as children and young people, the measures outlined in this chapter would mark important steps to true participatory governance.

References

Adam, B. (1995) *Timewatch: The Social Analysis of Time*. Polity Press, Cambridge.

Adams, E. and Ingham, S. (1998) *Changing Places: Children's Participation in Environmental Planning*. The Children's Society, London.

Adler, P. and Adler, P. (1994) Social reproduction and the corporate other: The institutionalization of after school activities. *Sociological Quarterly*, 35, 309–328.

Aitken, S. (1994) *Children's Geographies*. Association of American Geographers, Washington DC.

Aitken, S. (2001) *Geographies of Young People: The Morally Contested Spaces of Identity*. Routledge, London.

Aitken, S. and Ginsberg, S. (1988) Children's characterization of place. *Yearbook of the Association of Pacific Coast Geographers*, 50, 67–84.

Aitken, S. and Herman, T. (1997) Gender, power and crib geography: traditional spaces and potential places. *Gender, Place and Culture*, 4, 63–88.

Alanen, L. (1990) Rethinking socialization, the family and childhood. *Sociological Studies of Child Development*, 3, 13–28.

Alderson, P. (1995) *Listening to Children: Children, Ethics and Social Research*. Barnardos, Ilford.

Alderson, P. and Goodwin M. (1993) Contradictions within concepts of children's competence. *International Journal of Children's Rights*, 1, 303–313.

Ambert, A. (1994) An international perspective on parenting: social change and social constructs. *Journal of Marriage and the Family*, 56, 529–43.

Anderson, B. (1983) *Imagined Communities: Reflections on the Origin and Spread of Nationalism*. Verso, London.

Archard, D. (1993) *Children: Rights and Childhood*. Routledge, London.

Aries, P. (1962) *Centuries of Childhood: A Social History of Family Life*. Random House, New York.

Bannerjee, N. (1994) Curfews spread, but effects are still not clear. *The Wall Street Journal*, 4 March, p. 5.

Barnardos (1994) *The Facts of Life: The Changing Face of Childhood*. Barnardos, London.

Barnardos (1996) *Young People's Social Attitudes*. Barnardos, London.

Bartlett, S., Hart, R., Satterthwaite, D., La Barra, X. and Missair, A. (1999) *Cities For Children: Children's Rights, Poverty and Urban Management*. Earthscan Publications Limited, London.

Baumgartner, M. (1988) *The Moral Order of a Suburb*. Oxford University Press, New York.

BBC (2004) Net blamed for rise in child porn. http://news.bbc.co.uk/1/technology/3387377.stm Accessed 15 January 2004.

Beck, U. (1992) *Risk Society: Towards a New Modernity*. Sage, London.

Beck, U. and Beck-Gernsheim, E. (1995) *The Normal Chaos of Love*. Polity Press, Cambridge.

Beck, U. and Beck-Gernsheim, E. (2002) *Individualization*. Sage, London.

Bell, M. (1992) The fruit of difference: the rural-urban continuum as a system of identity. *Rural Sociology*, 57, 65–82.

Berman, M. (1986) Take it to the streets: conflict and community in public space, *Dissent*, Fall, 470–94.

Bernardes, J. (1987) 'Doing things with words': sociology and 'family policy' debates. *Sociological Review*, 36, 267–72.

Bigner, J. (1974) Second borns' discrimination of sibling role concepts. *Developmental Psychology*, 10, 564–573.

Bjorklid, P. (1985) Children's outdoor environment from the perspective of environmental and development psychology, in Gartling, T. and Vaalsiner, J. (eds) *Children Within Environments: Towards a Psychology of Accident Prevention*. Plenum, New York.

Blakeley, K. (1994) Parents' conceptions of social dangers to children in the urban environment. *Children's Environments*, 11, 16–25.

Blaut, J. (1971) Space, structure and maps. *Tijdschrift voor Economische en Sociale Geografie*, 62, 1–4.

Blaut, J. and Stea, D. (1974) Mapping at the age of three. *Journal of Geography*, 73, 5–9.

Blitzer, S. (1991) They are only children, what do they know? A look at current ideologies of childhood. *Sociological Studies of Child Development*, 4, 11–25.

Boethius, U. (1995) Youth, the media and moral panics in Fornas, J. and Bolin, G. (eds) *Youth Culture in Late Modernity*. Sage, London.

Boulton, M. (1983) *On Being a Mother: A Study of Women with Preschool Children*. Tavistock, London.

Bowlby, J. (1969) *Attachment and Loss*. Penguin, Harmondsworth.

Brah, A. (1993) 'Race' and 'culture' in the gendering of labour markets: South Asian young Muslim women and the labour market. *New Community*, 19, 441–458.

Brannen, J. and Moss, P. (1988) *New Mothers at Work*. Unwin, London.

Breitbart, M. (1998) Dana's mystical tunnel: young people's designs for survival and change in the city, in Skelton, T. and Valentine, G. (eds) *Cool Places: Geographies of Youth Cultures*. Routledge, London.

Brim, O. (1958) Family structure and sex role learning by children. *Sociometry*, 21, 1–16.

Buchner, P. (1990) Growing up in the Eighties: changes in the social biography of childhood in the FRG, in Chisholm, L., Buchner, P., Kruger,

H.H. and Brown, P. (eds) *Childhood, Youth and Social Change: A Comparative Perspective*. Falmer Press, London.

Bunge, W.W. (1977) The point of reproduction: a second front. *Antipode*, 9, 60–76.

Butler, J. (1990) *Gender Troubles: Feminism and the Subversion of Identity*. Routledge, London.

Cahill, S. (1990) Childhood and public life: reaffirming biographical divisions. *Social Problems*, 37, 390–402.

Cahill, S. (2000) Street literacy: urban teenagers' strategies for negotiating their neighbourhood. *Journal of Youth Studies*, 3, 251–277.

Cameron, D. and Fraser, L. (1987) *Lust to Kill: A Feminist Investigation of Sexual Murder*. University Press, New York.

Campbell, J. (1993) US teens face curfew to beat crime, *Evening Standard*, 30 November, p. 3.

Caputo, V. (1995) Anthropology's silent others in Amit-Talai, V. and Wulff, H. (eds) *Youth Cultures: A Cross-Cultural Perspective*. Routledge, London.

Castellani, G. (1997) The Italian experience of children's councils. Paper presented at the Congress of Local and Regional Authorities of Europe. Budapest, October.

Chawla, L. (2002) (ed.) *Growing Up in an Urbanising World*. Earthscan Publications and UNESCO, London.

Chandler, J. (1991) *Women Without Husbands: An Exploration of the Margins of Marriage*. Macmillan, Basingstoke.

Chodorow, N. and Contratto, S. (1982) The fantasy of the perfect mother, in Thorne, B. and Yalom, M. (eds) *Rethinking the Family: Some Feminist Questions*. Longman, London.

Cloke, P., Philo, C. and Sadler, D. (1991) *Approaching Human Geography*. Paul Chapman, London.

Cohen, S. (1972) *Folk Devils and Moral Panics: The Creation of Mods and Rockers*. MacGibbon and Kee, London.

Collins, D. and Kearns, R.A. (2001) Under curfew and under siege? Legal geographies of young people, *Geoforum*, 32, 389–403.

Corrigan, P. (1979) *Schooling the Smash Street Kids*. Macmillan, Basingstoke.

Cream, J. (1993) Child abuse and the symbolic geographies of Cleveland. *Environment and Planning D: Society and Space*, 11, 231–246.

Davis, M. (1990) *City of Quartz*. Vintage, London.

Department of the Environment (1973) *Children at Play*. HMSO, London.

Diduck, A. (1999) Justice and childhood: reflections on refashioning boundaries in King, M. (ed.) *Moral Agendas for Children's Welfare*. Routledge, London.

Donaldson, M. (1978) *Children's Minds*. Fontana, London.

Douglas, M. (1992) *Risk and Blame: Essays in Cultural Theory*. Routledge, London.

Dowling, R. (2000) Cultures of mothering and car use in suburban Sydney: a preliminary investigation. *Geoforum*, 31, 345–53.

Downey, D., Braboy, J.P. and Powell, B. (1994) Sons versus daughters: sex composition of children and maternal views on socialization. *The Sociological Quarterly*, 35, 33–50.

Dumm, T.L. (1994) The new enclosures: racism in the normalised community, in Gooding-Williams, R. (ed.) *Reading Rodney King/Reading Urban Uprising*. Routledge, London.

Dyck, I. (1989a) Integrating home and wage workplace: women's daily lives in a Canadian suburb. *The Canadian Geographer*, 33, 329–41.

Dyck, I. (1989b) A home away from home: women's changing activities and informal day-care solutions. *Ohio Geographer*, 17, 100–117.

Dyck, I. (1990) Space, time, and renegotiating motherhood: an exploration of the domestic workplace. *Environment and Planning D: Society and Space*, 8, 459–483.

Eden, K. and Roker, D. (2000) 'You've gotta do something ...': a longitudinal study of young people's involvement in social action. Paper presented at ESRC Youth Research 2000 Conference, University of Keele.

Elliott, M. (1988) Caring about safety. *Social Work Today*, 19, 25–26.

Ellis, W. (1995) The death of childhood. *The Times*, 1 August, page 13.

Ennew, J. (1994) Time for children or time for adults?, in Qvortrup, J., Bardy, M., Sgritta, G. and Wintersberger, H. (eds) *Childhood Matters: Social Theory, Practice and Politics*. Avebury, Aldershot.

Epstein, D. (1993) Too small to notice? Constructions of childhood and discourse of 'race' in predominantly white contexts. *Curriculum Studies*, 1, 317–334.

Etzioni, A. (1993) *The Spirit of Community: The Reinvention of American Society*. Simon & Schuster, New York.

Fielding, S. (2000) Walk on the left! Children's geographies and the primary school, in Holloway, S.L. and Valentine, G. (eds) *Children's Geographies: Playing, Living, Learning*. Routledge, London.

Finch, J. and Mason, J. (1993) *Negotiating Family Responsibilities*. Routledge, London.

Flekkoy, M.G. (1995) The Scandinavian experience of children's rights, in Franklin, B. (ed.) *A Handbook of Children's Rights: Comparative Policy and Practice*. Routledge, London.

Foreign and Commonwealth Office (2004) Drugs and international crime. http://www.fco.gov.uk/servlet/front?pagename=OpenMarket/Xcelerate/ Show Accessed 16 January 2004.

Franklin, B. (ed.) *A Handbook of Children's Rights: Comparative Policy and Practice*. Routledge, London.

Franklin, B. and Petley, J. (1996) Killing the age of innocence: newspaper reporting of the death of James Bulger in Pilcher, J. and Wagg, S. (eds) *Thatcher's Children: Politics, Childhood and Society in the 1980s and 1990s*. Falmer Press, London.

Freeman, C. (1996) Local Agenda 21 as a vehicle for encouraging children's participation in environmental planning. *Local Government Policy Making*, 23, 45–51.

Freeman, C., Nairn, K. and Sligo, J. (2003) 'Professionalising' participation: from rhetoric to practice. *Children's Geographies*, 1, 53–70.

Furlong, A. and Cartmel, F. (1997) *Young People and Social Change*. Open University Press, Buckingham.

Fyfe, N. and Bannister, J. (1998) 'The eyes upon the street': closed-circuit television surveillance and the city, in Fyfe, N. (ed.) *Images of the Street*. Routledge, London.

Gagen, E.A. (1998) 'An example to us all': children's bodies and identity construction in early twentieth century playgrounds. Paper presented at the Geographies of Young People and Young People's Geographies Workshop, San Diego State University, November.

Gagen, E.A. (2000) Playing the part: performing gender in America's playgrounds, in Holloway, S.L. and Valentine, G. (eds) *Children's Geographies: Playing, Living, Learning*. Routledge, London.

Gergen, K.J., Gloger-Tippelt, G. and Berkowitz, P. (1990) The cultural construction of the developing child, in Semin, G.R. and Gergen, K.J. (eds) *Everyday Understandings: Social and Scientific Understanding*. Sage, London.

Gibson, J.J. (1979) *The Ecological Approach to Visual Perception*. Loughton and Mifflin, Boston.

Giddens, A. (1991) *Modernity and Self Identity*. Polity Press, Cambridge.

Goldson, B. (1997) Children in trouble: state responses to juvenile crime, in Scraton, P. (ed.) *Childhood in Crisis*. UCL Press, London.

Gordon, L. (1982) Why nineteenth-century feminists did not support 'birth control' and twentieth-century feminists do: feminism, reproduction, and the family, in Thorne, B. and Yalom, M. (eds) *Rethinking the Family: Some Feminist Questions*. Longman, London.

Gordon, M.T. and Heath, L. (1981) The news business, crime and fear, in Lewis D. (ed.) *Reactions to Crime*. Sage, Beverley.

Graham, S. (1998) Spaces of surveillant simulation: new technologies, digital representations and material geographies. *Environment and Planning D: Society and Space*, 16, 483–504.

Gregson, N. and Lowe, M. (1993) Renegotiating the domestic division of labour? A study of dual career households in north east and south east England. *The Sociological Review*, 41, 3, 475–505.

Grimm-Thomas, K. and Perry-Jenkins, I. (1994) All in a days work: job experiences, self-esteem and fathering in working class families. *Family Relations*, 43, 174–181.

Gullone, E. and King, N. (1993) The fears of youth in the 1990s: contemporary normative data. *Journal of Genetic Psychology*, 154, 137–153.

Hardyment, C. (1990) Mum's the word no more. *The Guardian*, 3 November, p. 8.

Harper, S. (1989) The British rural community: an overview of perspectives. *Journal of Rural Studies*, 5, 2 ,161–184.

Harris, C. (1983) *The Family and Industrial Society*. Allen Unwin, London.

Hart, C. and Robinson, C. (1994) Comparative study of maternal and paternal disciplinary strategies. *Psychological Reports*, 74, 495–498.

Hart, R. (1979) *Children's Experience of Place*. Irvington, New York.

Hart, R. (1992) Children's participation in planning and design in Altman, L. and Low, S.L. (eds) *Place Attachment: Human Behaviour and Environment Advances in Theory and Research*, 12. New York, Plenum.

Hart, R. (1997) *Children's Participation: The Theory and Practice of Involving Young Citizens in Community Development and Environmental Care*. UNICEF/Earthscan Publications, London.

Hart, R. and Schwab, M. (1997) Children's rights and the building of democracy: a dialogue on the international movement for children's participation. *Social Justice*, 24, 177–191.

Hebdige, D. (1988) *Hiding in the Light*. Routledge, London.

Hendrick, H. (1990) Constructing and reconstructions of British childhood: an interpretative survey, 1800 to present, in James, A. and Prout, A. (eds) *Constructing and Reconstructing Childhood: Contemporary Issues in the Sociological Study of Children*. Falmer Press, Basingstoke.

Herbert, S. (1998) Policing contested space: on patrol at Smiley and Hauser, in Fyfe, N. (ed.) *Images of the Street*. Routledge, London.

Hesse, B., Rai, D.K., Bennett, C. and McGilchrist, P. (1992) *Young People's Leisure and Lifestyles*. Routledge, London.

Hillman, M., Adams J. and Whitelegg J. (1990) *One False Move ... A Study of Children's Independent Mobility*, Policy Studies Institute, London.

Hodgkin, R. (1998) Crime and disorder bill. *Children and Society*, 12, 66–68.

Hodgkin, R. and Newell, P. (1996) *Effective Government Structures for Children*. Calouste Gulbenkian Foundation, London.

Holden, G. and Zambarano, R. (1992) Passing the rod: similarities between parents and their young children in orientations toward physical punishment, in Siegel, I., McGillicuddy-Delisi, I. and Goodnow, J. (eds) *Parental Belief Systems: The Psychological Consequences for Children*. Erlbaum, Hillsdale NJ.

Holloway, S.L. (1998) Local childcare cultures: moral geographies of mothering and the social organisation of pre-school education. *Gender, Place and Culture*, 5, 29–53.

Holloway, S.L. and Valentine, G. (2000) Spatiality and the new social studies of childhood, *Sociology*, 34, 763–783.

Holloway, S.L. and Valentine, G. (2001a) 'It's only as stupid as you are': children and adults' negotiation of ICT competence at home and at school. *Social and Cultural Geography*, 2, 25–42.

Holloway, S.L. and Valentine, G. (2001b) Children at home in the wired world: reshaping and rethinking the home in urban geography. *Urban Geography*, 22, 562–83.

Holloway, S.L. and Valentine, G. (2003) *Cyberkids: Children in the Information Age*. RoutledgeFalmer, London.

Holloway, S.L., Valentine, G. and Bingham, N. (2000) Institutionalising technologies: masculinities, femininities and the heterosexual economy of the IT classroom. *Environment and Planning A*, 32, 617–33.

Holt, J. (1975) *Escape From Childhood*. Penguin, Harmondsworth.

Hood, S., Kelley, P., Mayall, B. and Oakley, A. (1996) *Children. Parents and Risk*. Social Science Research Unit. Institute of Education, London.

Hood Williams, J. (1990) Patriarchy for children: on the stability of power relations in children's lives, in Chisholm, L., Buchner, P., Herman-Kruger, H. and Brown, P. (eds) *Childhood, Youth and Social Change: a Comparative Perspective*. Falmer Press, Basingstoke.

Hungerford, H.R. and Volk, T.L. (1990) Changing learner behaviour through Environmental Education. *Journal of Environmental Education*, 21, 8–21.

Jacobs, J. (1961) *The Death and Life of Great American Cities*. Random House Inc., New York.

Jackson, S. (1996) Ignorance is bliss when you're just seventeen. *Trouble and Strife*, 33, 36–40.

Jackson, S. and Scott, S. (1999) Risk anxiety and the social construction of childhood, in Lupton, D. (ed.) *Risk and Socialcultural Theory*. Cambridge University, Cambridge.

James, A. and Jenks, C. (1996) Public perceptions of childhood criminality, *British Journal of Sociology*, 47, 315–331.

James, A. and Prout, A. (1990) (eds) *Constructing and Reconstructing Childhood: Contemporary Issues in the Sociological Study of Childhood*. Falmer Press, London.

Jamison, A. and Gilbert L. (2000) Facilitating children's voices in the community and government in Smith, A.B., Taylor, N. and Gollop, M. (eds) *Children's Voices: Research Policy and Practice*. Longman, Auckland.

Jamieson, L. and Toynbee, C. (1989) Shifting patterns of parental authority, 1900–1980, in Corr, L. and Jamieson, H. (eds) *The Politics of Everyday Life*. Macmillan, London.

Jeffs, T. and Smith, M. (1996) Getting the dirt bags off the street. *Youth and Policy*, 53, 1–14.

Jenks, C. (1996) *Childhood*. Routledge, London.

Jensen, A.M. (1994) The feminization of childhood, in Qvortrup, J., Bardy, M., Sgritta, G. and Wintersberger, H. (eds) *Childhood Matters: Social Theory, Practice and Politics*. Avebury Press, Aldershot.

Jodry, C. (1997) Youth participation and the role of ANACEJ. Paper presented at the Congress of Local and Regional Authorities of Europe. Budapest, October.

Jones, O. (1997) Little figures, big shadows, country childhood stories, in Cloke, P. and Little, J. (eds) *Contested Countryside Cultures*. Routledge, London.

Jones, O. (2000) Melting geography: purity, disorder, childhood and space, in Holloway, S.L. and Valentine, G. (eds) *Children's Geographies: Playing, Living, Learning*. Routledge, London.

Jordanova, L. (1989) Children in history: concepts of nature and society, in Scarre, G. (ed.) *Children, Parents and Politics*. Cambridge University Press, Cambridge.

Karsten, l. (1998) Growing up in Amsterdam: Differentiation and segregation in children's lives. *Urban Studies*, 35, 565–581.

Katz, C. (1991) Sow what you know: the struggle for social reproduction in Rural Sudan. *Annals of the Association of American Geographers*, 8, 488–514.

Katz, C. (1993) Growing girls/closing circles: limits on the spaces of knowing in rural Sudan and US cities, in Katz, C. and Monk, J. (eds) *Full Circles: Geographies of Women Over the Life Course*. Routledge, London.

Katz, C. (1994) Textures of global change: eroding ecologies of childhood in New York and Sudan, *Childhood*, 2, 103–110.

Katz, C. (1995) Power, space and terror: social reproduction and the public environment. Paper presented at the Landscape Architecture, Social Ideology and the Politics of Place Conference, Harvard University, Massachusetts.

Katz, C. (1998) Disintegrating developments: global economic restructuring and the eroding of ecologies of youth in Skelton, T. and Valentine, G. (eds) *Cool Places: Geographies of Youth Cultures*. Routledge, London.

Keith M. (1995) Making the street visible: placing racial violence in context. *New Community*, 21, 551–565.

Kelley, P., Hood, S. and Mayall, B. (1998) Children, parents and risk. *Health and Social care in the Community*, 6, 16–24.

Kelley, P., Mayall, B. and Hood, S. (1997) Children's accounts of risk. *Childhood*, 4, 305–24.

Kitizinger, J. (1990) Who are you kidding? Children, power and the struggle against sexual abuse, in Prout, A. and James, A. (eds) *Constructing and Reconstructing Childhood*. Falmer Press, Basingstoke.

Klayman, J. (1985) Children's decision strategies and their adaptation to task characteristics. *Organization Behaviour and Human Decision Processes*, 35, 179–201.

Lamb, M. (1987) Introduction: the emergent American father, in Lamb, M. (ed.) *The Father's Role: Cross Cultural Perspectives*. Lawrence Erlbaum, Hillsdale, NJ.

Lamb, M. and Sutton-Smith, S. (1982) *Sibling Relationships: their Nature and Significance Across the Lifespan*. Lawrence Erlbaum, Hillsdale, NJ.

Lansdown, G. (1995) *Taking Part: Children's Participation in Decision Making*. Institute of Public Policy Research, London).

Larossa, R. (1988) Fatherhood and social change. *Family Relations*, 37, 451–457.

Lester, B.J. (1996) Is it too late for juvenile curfews? Qutb logic and the constitution. *Hofstra Law Review*, 25, 665–701.

Ley, D. and Cybriwsky, R. (1974) Urban graffiti as territorial markers. *Annals of the Association of American Geographers*, 64, 491–505.

Lieberg, M. (1995) Teenagers and public space. *Communication Research*, 22, 720–44.

Lister, R. (1997) *Citizenship: Feminist Perspectives*. New York University Press, New York.

Little J. and Austin, P. (1996) Women and the rural idyll, in Cloke, P. and Little, J. (eds) *Contested Countryside Cultures: Rurality and Socio-Cultural Marginalisation*. Routledge, London.

Lucas, T. (1998) Youth gangs and moral panics in Santa Cruz, California, in Skelton, T. and Valentine G. (eds) *Cool Places: Geographies of Youth Cultures*. Routledge, London.

Ludescher, M. (1997) The Swiss youth parliament movement. Paper presented at the Congress of Local and Regional Authorities of Europe. Budapest, October.

Lynch, K. (1979) *Growing Up in Cities*. MIT Press, Cambridge, MA.

Massey, D. (1993) Power-geometry and a progressive sense of place in Bird, J., Curtis, B., Putnam, T. Robertson, G. and Tickner, L. (eds) *Mapping the Future: Local Cultures, Global Change*. Routledge, London.

Massey, D. (1998) The spatial construction of youth cultures in Skelton, T. and Valentine, G. (eds) *Cool Places: Geographies of Youth Cultures*. Routledge, London.

Massey, D. (1999) Spaces of politics, in Massey, D., Allen, J. and Sarre, P. (eds) *Human Geography Today*. Polity Press, Cambridge.

Marshall, T.H. (1950) *Citizenship and Social Class*. Cambridge University Press, Cambridge.

Marshall, H. (1991) The social construction of motherhood: an analysis of childcare and parenting manuals, in Phoenix, A., Woollett, A. and Lloyd, E. (eds) *Motherhood: Meanings, Practices and Ideologies*. Sage, London.

Matthews, M.H. (1987) Gender, home range and environmental cognition. *Transactions of the Institute of British Geography*, 12, 43–56.

Matthews, H. (1995) Living on the edge: children as 'outsiders'. *Tijdschrift voor Economische en Sociale Geografie*, 86, 456–466.

Matthews, H. and Limb, M. (1998) The right to say: the development of youth councils/forums within the UK. *Area*, 30, 66–78.

Matthews, H., Limb, M. and Taylor, M. (1999a) Reclaiming the street: the discourse of curfew. *Environment and Planning A*, 31, 1713–1730.

Matthews, H., Limb, M. and Taylor, M. (1999b) Young people's participation and representation in society. *Geoforum*, 30, 135–144.

May, M. (1973) Innocence and experience: the evolution of the concept of juvenile delinquency in the mid-19th century, *Victorian Studies* 17, 7–29.

Mayall, B. (ed.) (1994) *Children's Childhoods Observed and Experienced*. Falmer Press, Basingstoke.

McKendrick, J.H., Fielder, A.V. and Bradford, M.G. (1999) Privatisation of collective playspaces in the UK. *Built Environment*, 25, 44–57.

McKendrick, J.H., Bradford, M.G. and Fielder, A.V. (2000) Time for a party! Making sense of the commercialisation of leisure space for children in Holloway, S.L. and Valentine, G. (eds) *Children's Geographies: Playing, Living, Learning* Routledge, London.

McNeish, D. and Roberts, H. (1995) *Playing It Safe: Today's Children at Play* Barnardo's, Essex.

McRobbie, A. (1994) Folk devils fight back. *New Left Review*, 203, 107–116.

Medrich, E., Roizen, J., Rubin, V. and Buckley, S. (1982) *The Serious Business of Growing Up*. University California Press, Berkeley.

Mercer, C. (1976) *Living in Cities: Psychology and the Urban Environment*. Penguin, Harmondsworth.

Mitchell, D. (1995) The end of public space? People's Park, definitions of the public and democracy. *Annals of the Association of American Geographers*, 85, 108–33.

Mitchell, D. (1996) Political violence, order, and the legal construction of public space: power and the public forum doctrine. *Urban Geography*, 17, 158–78.

Moore, R.C. (1986) *Childhood's Domain: Play and Place in Child Development*. Croom Helm, Beckenham.

Morgan, D.H.J. (1996) *Family Connections*. Cambridge, Polity Press.

Morial, M. (1995) Our juvenile curfew is working. *National Cities Weekly*, 18, 5–8.

Morley, D. (1986) *Family Television: Cultural Power and Domestic Leisure*. Comedia, London.

Morrow, V. (1994) Responsible children? Aspects of children's work and employment outside school in contemporary UK, in Mayall, B. (ed.) *Children's Childhoods Observed and Experienced*. Falmer Press, Basingstoke.

Morrow, V. and Richards, M. (1996) The ethics of social research on children: an overview. *Children & Society*, 10, 90–105.

Nasman, E. (1994) Individualisation and institutionalisation of childhood in today's Europe in Qvortrup, J., Bardy M., Sgritta, S. and Wintersberger, H. (eds) *Childhood Matters: Social Theory, Practice and Politics*. Avebury, Aldershot.

Nesmith C. and Radcliffe S. (1993) (Re)Mapping Mother Earth: a geographical perspective on environmental feminisms. *Environment and Planning D: Society and Space*, 11, 375–496.

Newson, J. and Newson, E. (1976) *Seven Years Old in the Home Environment* Hutchinson, London.

National Criminal Intelligence Service (2002) Paedophile crime, including on-line child abuse. http://www.ncis.co.uk/ukta/2002/threat9.asp Accessed 15 January 2004.

NSPCC (2000) Survey finds hidden victims of child abuse. http://www.nspcc.org.uk/html/home/informationresources/hiddenchildabuses Accessed 16 January 2004.

NSPCC (2004) Facts and figures about child abuse. http://www.nspcc.org.uk/ html/home/newsandcampaigns/factsandfigures.htm Accessed 16 January 2004.

Norris, C. and Armstrong, G. (1997) *Categories of Control: the Social Construction of Suspicion and Intervention in CCTV Systems*. Report to the ESRC. Copy available from the Dept. of Social Policy, University of Hull, Hull, UK.

Office of Juvenile Justice and Delinquency Prevention (1996) Curfew: an answer to juvenile delinquency and victimisation? *Juvenile Justice Bulletin* (April), 1–5.

Oldman, D. (1994a) Childhood as a mode of production, in Mayall, B. (ed.) *Children's Childhoods Observed and Experienced*. Falmer Press, London.

Oldman, D. (1994b) Adult-child relations as class relations in Qvortrup, J., Bardy, M., Sgritta, G. and Wintersberger, H. (eds) *Childhood Matters: Social Theory, Practice and Politics*. Avebury Press, Aldershot.

Opie, I. and Opie, E. (1969) *Children's Games in Streets and Playgrounds*. Oxford University Press, London.

O'Toole, T. (2003) Engaging with Young People's Conceptions of the Political. *Children's Geographies*, 1, 71–90.

Parkinson, C. (1987) *Children's Range Behaviour*. Playboard, Birmingham.

Pearson, G. (1983) *Hooligan: A History of Respectable Fears*. Macmillan, London.

Percy-Smith, B. and Matthews, H. (2001) Tyrannical spaces: young people, bullying and urban neighbourhoods. *Local Environment*, 6, 49–63.

Perez, C. and Hart, R. (1980) Beyond playgrounds: planning for children's access to the environment, in Wilkinson, P. (ed.) *Innovations in Play Environments*. Croom Helm, London.

Perloff, L. (1983) Perceptions of vulnerability to victimisation *Journal of Social Issues*, 39, 41–61.

Peterson, L., Ewigman, B. and Vandiver, T. (1994) Role of Parental Anger in Low-income Women: Discipline Strategy, Perceptions of Behaviour Problems and the Need for Control. *Journal of Clinical Child Psychology*, 23, 435–443.

Philo, C.J. (1997) Of other rurals, in Cloke, P. and Little, J. (eds) *Contested Countryside Cultures*. Routledge, London.

Philo, C.J. (2003) 'To go back up the side hill': memories, imaginations and reveries of childhood. *Children's Geographies*, 1, 7–24.

Phoenix, A. and Woollett, A. (1991) Motherhood: social construction, politics and psychology, in Phoenix, A., Woollett, A. and Lloyd, E. (eds) *Motherhood: Meanings, Practices and Ideologies*. Sage, London.

Piaget, J. (1952) *The Origins of Intelligence in Children*. Translated by Marjorie Worden. Harcourt, Brace and World Inc., New York.

Piaget, J. (1971) *Structuralism*. Translated by Chaninah Maschler. Basic Books, New York.

Pilkington, E. (1994) 'Killing the age of innocence', *The Guardian*, 30 May, p. 18.

Ploszajska, T. (1994) Moral landscapes and manipulated spaces: gender, class and space in Victorian reformatory schools. *Journal of Historical Geography*, 20, 413–429.

Plotkin, A. and Elias, G. (1977) The Curfew Bill as it relates to the juvenile and his family. *Adolescence*, 12, 48–52.

Popenoe, D. (1988) *Disturbing the Nest: Family Change and Decline in Modern Societies*. De Gruyter, New York.

Postman, N. (1982) *The Disappearance of Childhood*. Delacourt Press, New York.

Prout, A. and James, A. (1990) A new paradigm for the sociology of childhood? Provenance, promise and problems, in James A. and Prout, A. (eds) *Constructing and Reconstructing Childhood: Contemporary Issues in the Sociological Study of Childhood*. Falmer Press, Basingstoke.

Quadrel, M.J., Fischhoff, B. and Davis, W. (1993) Adolescent (In)vulnerability *American Psychologist*, 48, 102–116.

Qvortrup, J. (1994) Childhood matters: an introduction in Qvortrup, J., Bardy, M., Sgritta, G. and Wintersberger, H. (eds) *Childhood Matters: Social Theory, Practices and Politics*. Avebury Press, Aldershot.

Riechmann, D. (1997) A growing number of US cities are using nighttime and daytime youth curfews. *Detroit News*, 1 January, p. 5.

Rosenbaum, M. (1993) *Children and Environment*. National Children's Bureau, London.

Rosenbaum, M. and Newell, P. (1991) *Taking Children Seriously: A Proposal for a Children's Rights Commissioner*. Calouste Gulbenkian Foundation, London.

Roberts, H., Smith, S.J. and Lloyd, M. (1992) Safety as a social value: A community approach. Scott, S., Williams, G., Platt, S. and Thomas, H. (eds) *Private Risks and Public Dangers*. Avebury, Aldershot.

Robertson, G. (1976) Home as a nest: middle class childhood in nineteenth century Europe. In DeMause, L. (ed.) *The History of Childhood*. Souvenir Press, London.

Rose, G. (1990) Imagining Poplar in the 1920s: contested concepts of community. *Journal of Historical Geography*, 16, 425–437.

Ruddick, S. (1982) Maternal Thinking, in Thorne, B. and Yalom, M. (eds) *Rethinking the Family: Some Feminist Questions*. Longman, London.

Saegert, S. and Hart, R. (1978) The development of environmental competence in girls and boys, in Salter, M. (ed.) *Play: Anthropological Perspectives*. Leisure Press, New York.

Satterthwaite, D., Hart, R., Levy, L., Mitlin, D., Ross, D., Smit, J. and Stephens, C. (1996) *The Environment for Children: Understanding and Acting on the Environmental Hazards That Threaten Children and Their Parents*. Earthscan, London.

Schiraldi, V. (1996) Curfew laws: no panacea for juvenile crime. *Bulletin of the Center of Juvenile and Criminal Justice* (January) 1–2.

Schnell, R. (1979) Childhood as ideology: a reinterpretation of the common school. *British Journal of Educational Studies*, xxvII, 7–28.

Scott, S., Jackson, S. and Backett-Milburn, K. (1998) Swings and round-abouts: risk anxiety and the everyday worlds of children. *Sociology*, 32, 689–705.

Scott, S. and Watson-Brown, L. (1997) The beast, the family and the innocent children. *Trouble and Strife*, 36, 36–40.

Seabrook, J. (1987) The decay of childhood. *New Statesman*, 10 July, 14–15.

Seamon, D. (1979) *A Geography of the Lifeworld*. Croom Helm, London.

Sennett, R. (1993) *The Fall of Public Man*. Faber and Faber, London.

Sennett, R. (1996) *The Uses of Disorder: Personal Identity and City Life*. Faber and Faber, London.

Shoard, M. (1980) *The Theft of the Countryside*. Maurice Temple-Smith, London.

Short, J. (1991) *Imagined Country: Society, Culture and Environment*. Routledge, London.

Sibley, D. (1988) Survey 3: Purification of space. *Environment and Planning D: Society and Space*, 6, 409–21.

Sibley, D. (1991) Children's geographies: some problems of representation, *Area*, 23, 269–70.

Sibley, D. (1995a) Families and domestic routines: constructing the boundaries of childhood in Pile, S. and Thrift, N. (eds) *Mapping the Subject*. Routledge, London.

Sibley, D. (1995b) *Geographies of Exclusion: Society and Difference in the West*. Routledge, London.

Silk, J. (1999) The dynamics of community, place and identity. *Environment and Planning A*, 31, 5–17.

Silva, E.B. and Smart, C. (1999) 'The 'new' practices and politics of family life, in Silva, E.B. and Smart, C. (eds) *The New Family*. Sage, London.

Skelton, T. (2000) 'Nothing to do, nowhere to go?': teenage girls and 'public' space in the Rhondda Valley, South Wales, in Holloway, S.L. and Valentine, G. (eds) *Children's Geographies: Playing, Living, Learning*. Routledge, London.

Smart, C. (1999) The 'new' parenthood: fathers and mothers after divorce, in Silva, E.B. and Smart, C. (eds) *The New Family*. Sage, London.

Smith, A.B. (2003, in press) Interpreting and supporting participation rights: contributions from sociocultural theory. *International Journal of Children's Rights*.

Smith, F.M. and Barker, J. (1999) *The Childcare Revolution: Facts and Figures*. Kids' Club Network, London.

Smith, F.M. and Barker, J. (2000) 'Out of school', in school: a social geography of out of school childcare, in Holloway, S.L. and Valentine, G. (eds) *Children's Geographies: Playing, Living, Learning*. Routledge, London.

Smith, N. (1990) *Uneven Development: Nature, Capital and The Production of Space*. Basil Blackwell, Oxford.

Smith, N. (1992) New City, New Frontier: the Lower East Side as Wild, Wild West in Sorkin, M. (ed.) *Variations on a Theme Park: the New American City and the End of Public Space*. Hill and Wang, New York.

Smith, S.J. (1984) Crime in the news. *British Journal of Criminology*, 24, 289–95.

Smith, S.J. (1989) Society, space and citizenship: a human geography for 'new times'. *Transactions of the Institute of British Geographers*, 14, 144–56.

Solberg, A. (1990) Negotiating childhood: changing constructions of age for Norwegian children, in James, A. and Prout, A. (eds) *Constructing and Reconstructing Childhood: Contemporary Issues in the Sociological Study of Childhood*. Falmer Press, Basingstoke.

Sommerville, J. (1982) *The Rise and Fall of Childhood*. Sage, London.

Sorkin, M. (1992) See you in Disneyland, in Sorkin, M. (ed.)*Variations on a Theme Park: the New American City and the End of Public Space*. Hill and Wang, New York.

Spitzer, N. (1986) The children's crusade. *Atlantic*, 257, June, 18–22.

Stables, J. and Smith, F. (1999) 'Caught in the Cinderella': narratives of disabled parents and carers, in Parr. H. and Butler, R. (eds) *Mind and Body Spaces: Geographies of Illness, Impairment and Disability*. Routledge, London.

Stacey, J. (1990) *Brave New Families: Stories of Domestic Upheaval in the Late Twentieth Century America*. Basic Books, New York.

Stainton Rogers, R. and Stainton Rogers, W. (1992) *Stories of Childhood: Shifting Agendas of Childhood*. Harvester Wheatsheaf, Hemel Hempstead.

Stanko, E. (1987) Typical violence, normal precaution: Men, women and interpersonal violence in England, Wales, Scotland and the USA. In Hanmer, J. and Maynard, M. (eds) *Women, Violence and Social Control*. Macmillan, Basingstoke.

Steedman, C. (1990) *Childhood, Culture and Class in Britain*. Virago, London.

Steedman, C. (1995) *Strange Dislocations: Childhood and the Idea of Human Interiority 1780–1930*. Virago, London.

Storrie, T. (1997) Citizens or what? In Roche, J. and Tucker, S. (eds) *Youth and Society*. Sage, London.

Takanishi, R. (1978) Childhood as a social issue: historical roots of contemporary child advocacy movements. *Journal of Social Issues*, 34, 8–27.

Thompson, L. and Walker, A. (1989) Gender in families: women and men in marriage, work and parenthood. *Journal of Marriage and the Family*, 51, 845–871.

Thorne, B. (1987) Revisioning women and social change: where are the children? *Gender and Society*, 1, 85–109.

Thorne, B. (1994) *Gender Play: Girls and Boys in School*. Rutgers University Press, N.J.

Tonnies, F. (1955) *Community and Society*. Harper Row, New York (original 1887).

Toon, I. and Qureshi, T. (1995) The contestation over residential and urban space in the Isle of Dogs. Paper presented at the British Sociology Association Annual Conference, University of Leicester.

Travis, A. (2003) On the spot fines to fight yob culture, *The Guardian*, 13 March p. 11.

Trollinger, T. (1996) The juvenile curfew: unconstitutional imprisonment. *William and Mary Bill of Rights Journal*, 4, 949–1003.

Tucker, F. (2003) Sameness or difference? Exploring girls' use of recreational space. *Children's Geographies*, 1, 111–124.

Tucker F. and Matthews, H. (2001) 'They don't like girls hanging around there'; conflicts over recreational space in rural Northamptonshire. *Area*, 33, 161–68.

Valentine, G. (1989) The geography of women's fear, *Area*, 21, 385–90.

Valentine, G. (1992) Images of danger: women's sources of information about the spatial distribution of male violence. *Area*, 24, 22–29.

Valentine, G. (1996a) Children should be seen and not heard: the production and transgression of adults' public space. *Urban Geography*, 17, 173–188.

Valentine, G. (1996b) Angels and devils: moral landscapes of childhood. *Environment and Planning D: Society and Space*, 14, 581–599.

Valentine, G. (1997a) 'My son's a bit dizzy.' 'My wife's a bit soft': gender, children and cultures of parenting. *Gender, Place and Culture*, 4, 37–62.

Valentine, G. (1997b) 'Oh yes I can'. 'Oh no you can't': children and parents' understandings of kids' competence to negotiate public space safely. *Antipode*, 29, 65–89.

Valentine, G. (1997c) A safe place to grow up? Parenting, perceptions of children's safety and the rural idyll. *Journal of Rural Studies*, 13, 137–148.

Valentine, G. (1999a) Doing household research: interviewing couples together and apart. *Area*, 31, 67–74.

Valentine, G. (1999b) Eating in: home, consumption and identity. *Sociological Review*, 47, 491–524.

Valentine, G. (1999c) Being seen and heard? The ethical complexities of working with children and young people at home and at school. *Ethics, Place and Environment*, 2, 141–155.

Valentine, G. (2001) *Social Geographies: Space and Society*. Pearson, Harlow.

Valentine, G. and Holloway, S.L. (2001) On-line dangers? Geographies of parents' fears for children's safety in cyberspace, *The Professional Geographer*, 53, 71–83.

Valentine, G. and Holloway, S.L. (2002) Cyberkids? Exploring children's identities and social networks in on-line and off-line worlds. *Annals of the Association of American Geographers*, 92, 302–19.

Valentine, G., Holloway, S.L. and Bingham, N. (2002) The digital generation? Children, ICT and the everyday nature of social exclusion, *Antipode*, 34, 296–315.

Valentine, G. and McKendrick, J. (1997) Children's outdoor play: exploring parental concerns about children's safety and the changing nature of childhood. *Geoforum*, 28, 219–235.

Vanderbeck, R. and Johnson, J. (2000) 'That's the only place where you can hang out': urban young people and the space of the mall. *Urban Geography*, 21, 5–25.

van Vliet, W. (1981) Neighbourhood evaluations of city and suburban children. *Journal of the American Planning Association*, 47, 458–67.

Waksler, F.C. (1986) Studying children: phenomenological insights. *Human Studies*, 8, 171–82.

Walkerdine, V. (1984) *The Mastery of Reason*. Routledge, London.

Walkerdine, V. and Lucey, H. (1989) *Democracy in the Kitchen: Regulating Mothers and Socialising Daughters*. Virago, London.

Waltzer, M. (1986) Public space: a discussion on the shape of our cities. *Dissent*, fall, 470–76.

Ward, C. (1978) *The Child in the City*. Architectural Press, London.

Ward, C. (1990) *The Child in the Country*. Bedford Square Press, London.

Warner, M. (1989) 'Into the Dangerous World' *Counterblast*. Chatto and Windus, London.

Watt P. and Stenson K. (1998) Going out and about: youth and space in a southern English town, in Skelton, T. and Valentine, G. (eds) *Geographies of Youth Cultures*. Routledge, London.

Webster, C. (1995a) Youth crime, victimisation and racial harassment: the Keighley crime survey. Available from: Centre for Research in Applied Community Studies, Bradford & Ilkley Community College.

Webster, C. (1995b) Local heroes: youth crime, victimisation and racial harassment. Paper presented at the British Criminology Conference, University of Loughborough, July.

Weeks, J., Donovan, C. and Heaphy, B. (1999) Everyday experiments: narratives of non-heterosexual relationships, in Silva, E.B. and Smart, C. (eds) *The New Family*. Sage, London.

Weeks, J., Donovan, C. and Heaphy, B. (eds) (2000) *Same Sex Intimacies: Families of Choice and Other Life Experiments*. Routledge, London.

Westwood, S. (1990) Racism, black masculinity and the politics of space, in Hearn, J. and Morgan, D. (eds) *Men, Masculinities and Social Theory*. Unwin Hyman, London.

White, R. (2001) Youth participation in designing public places. *Youth Studies Australia*, 20, 19–26.

Willis, P. (1977) *Learning to Labour: How Working Class Kids Get Working Class Jobs*. London: Gower.

Wolfe M. (1978) Childhood and privacy. Altman, I. and Wohmill, J.F. *Children and the Environment*. Plenum Press, New York.

Woods, D. (1985a) Doing nothing. *Outlook*, 57, 3–20.

Woods, D. (1985b) Nothing doing. *Children's Environments Quarterly*, 7, 2–14.

Wood, D. and Beck, R. (1990) Dos and don'ts: family rules, rooms and their relationships. *Children's Environment Quarterly*, 7, 2–14.

Wood, D. and Beck, R. (1994) *The Home Rules*. John Hopkins Press, London.

Wyn, J. and White, R. (1997) *Rethinking Youth*. Sage, London.

Wyness, M. (1994) Keeping tabs on an uncivil society: positive parental control. *Sociology*, 28, 193–209.

Wyness, M. (1997) Parental responsibilities, social policy and the maintenance of boundaries. *Sociological Review*, 304–324.

Wyness, M. (2000) *Contesting Childhood*. Falmer Press, London.

Young, I.M. (1990) The ideal of community and the politics of difference, in Nicholson L.J. (ed.) *Feminism/Postmodernism*. Routledge, London.

Zill, N. (1983) *Summary of Preliminary Results: National Survey of Children*. Foundation for Child Development, New, York.

Zukin, S. (1995) *The Culture of Cities*. Blackwell, Oxford.

Index